Positive Body Image for Women

A Practical Guide to Foster Self Acceptance, Integrate Intuitive Eating and Break Free from Diet Culture

Lisa Ali, MA, LPC

Introduction
Welcome to your Journey

I have learned that my body is not an apology. It is a powerful, resilient being that deserves love and respect."
— Sonya Renee Taylor

It was a summer afternoon, and I stood in front of a full-length mirror, scrutinizing every inch of my body. I had just returned from a family gathering where everyone had an opinion about my appearance. "You've gained weight," one relative noted, while another offered unsolicited diet advice. I felt a familiar wave of shame wash over me. At that moment, I realized I had spent years trying to fit into an image that was never truly mine. The reflection staring back at me told a story of countless battles with self-acceptance, endless diets, and the exhausting pursuit of an impossible ideal.

This realization became the catalyst for change, not just in my own life, but in my mission to help others. This book is written for every woman who has stood in front of a mirror and felt like she wasn't enough. Its purpose is to empower you to foster self-acceptance, cultivate a positive body image, embrace intuitive eating, and break free from the chains of diet culture. This is more than just another self-help book—it's a holistic guide to wellness that respects your body, mind, and soul.

My journey with body acceptance and intuitive eating has been long and winding, and as I write this, it continues to evolve. As a licensed professional counselor, holistic healer, and energy mover, I have spent years helping women navigate their relationships with their bodies and food. But it wasn't until I faced my own issues head-on that I truly understood the depth of this struggle. I, too, have felt the pressure to conform to societal standards, experienced the anxiety, the self-doubt, and the isolation. Through this journey, I've discovered a path to healing and acceptance, and I'm here to share it with you.

Dear reader, I see you. I recognize the battles you fight every day —the feeling of not measuring up, the endless comparisons, and the harsh self-criticism. You are not alone. This book is your safe haven, a space to explore your relationship with your body and food without judgment. Here, you'll find empathy, understanding, and practical advice to guide you on this transformative journey.

This work is deeply rooted in inclusivity, embracing diverse perspectives on health, body size, and cultural norms. We will challenge the narrow definition of health being tied to a specific body type, and together, we'll explore ways to navigate social media and societal beauty standards without compromising your self-worth. Our goal is to help you feel at home in your skin and cultivate an empowering self-image that reflects your true essence.

As we begin this journey together, know that these pages have been thoughtfully crafted to walk beside you in your exploration of self-acceptance and healing. Think of this book as a gentle companion, one that honors your unique path and meets you exactly where you are. Each chapter unfolds like a conversation with a trusted friend, offering wisdom, gentle questions for reflection, and practical tools you can explore at your own pace.

While some of these ideas might feel familiar, others may offer new perspectives that illuminate your path in unexpected ways.

Remember that there's no "right way" to move through these pages. You might find yourself lingering in certain chapters, taking time to absorb and practice, while moving more quickly through others. This is perfectly natural and exactly as it should be.

Take what resonates, pause when you need to, and celebrate each small step forward. The intention here isn't to overwhelm but to empower, offering you tools and insights that can naturally weave into your daily life, honoring your personal pace and process.

So, I invite you to join me on this powerful journey of self-acceptance and empowerment. Commit to the exercises and reflections provided throughout the book, and embrace this opportunity to build a healthier, more positive relationship with your body, mind, and food. Let's walk this path together, honoring the diversity that makes us all beautifully unique.

Remember: You are more than enough; you are truly worthy, and you are not alone. Let's begin this journey to self-love and body positivity together.

Chapter 1

Understanding Body Image

"You alone are enough. You have nothing to prove to anybody."
— **Maya Angelou**

One weekday morning, I was in my favorite café, warming my hands around a steaming cup of coffee. Two young women sat at the table next to me, their voices carrying over the gentle hum of conversation. "I've tried everything," one sighed, "but I still can't fit into that dress size." My heart ached, remembering countless similar conversations with my clients, friends, and myself. These moments remind me why understanding body image is crucial to our self-acceptance journey.

As a counselor and someone who has walked this path, I've learned that body image is far more than what we see in the mirror. It's the story we tell ourselves about our bodies, the feelings that surge when we try on clothes, and the thoughts that whisper to us throughout the day. Let's explore this together with compassion and understanding.

Understanding Body Image: More Than Just a Reflection

In my years of counseling, I've noticed how often we reduce body image to what we see in the mirror. However, it's so much more complex and beautiful than that. Think of body image as a tapestry woven from multiple threads of our experience, how we perceive ourselves, what we feel about our bodies, our thoughts about our appearance, and the actions we take because of these feelings.

Let me share something personal: Early in my practice, I worked with a client who saw herself as "huge" despite being physically small. Her perception didn't match reality, but her feelings were absolutely real. This taught me something profound: body image isn't just about what we see; it's about how we experience our bodies in this world.

HERE's how I like to break it down:

1. Picture how you see yourself (**that's your perceptual body image**)
2. Notice what you feel about your body (**your emotional experience**)
3. Listen to your thoughts about your appearance (**your mental narrative**)
4. Observe how these feelings influence your actions (**your behavioral responses**)

You might be wondering about the difference between positive and negative body image. Think of it this way: Having a positive body image isn't about loving every inch of yourself every day, as that's not realistic. Instead, it's about having a true, kind perspective of your body without harsh distortions. It's about feeling comfortable in your skin, even on challenging days.

I remember standing in front of my own mirror years ago, battling negative body image. The journey from that place to where I am now taught me something vital: body image isn't fixed. It is like a river; it flows and changes. Some days, the current is gentle; others, it's turbulent. What matters is learning to navigate these waters with self-compassion.

Here is a little nugget of wisdom, you don't have to love your body to be at peace with it. This is where body neutrality comes in; a concept that has transformed many women's lives. Instead of focusing on loving how your body looks, what if we appreciate what it does for us? Your body carries you through life, helps you hug your loved ones, allows you to experience the world. Sometimes, acknowledging these simple truths can be more healing than striving for constant body positivity.

Remember, your relationship with your body is deeply personal and uniquely yours. As we continue this journey together, I invite you to approach these concepts with curiosity and gentleness. What resonates with you? What challenges you? Let's explore these questions together.

> **Reflection Moment:** *Take a quiet moment now. How do you typically speak to your body? If your body could write you a letter, what would it say? What would you say back?*

Looking Back: How History Shaped Our Body Stories

One afternoon, during a workshop I led, a participant asked me, "When did we start caring so much about how we look?" This question led me down a fascinating research path. Throughout history, our ideas about beauty and body image have shifted like sand dunes in the wind. What's considered "ideal" has never been static; it's always been influenced by culture, power, and social values. Let me take you on this journey through time. Picture yourself in Ancient Egypt, where beauty was about youth and symmetry. Fast-forward to the Renaissance, where paintings celebrated fuller figures and soft curves. These weren't just artistic choices; they reflected their times' deeper cultural values and social meanings.

But there's a more complex story here, one that we need to acknowledge. As European powers spread across the globe through colonialism, conquest, and eventually global media, they didn't just bring their languages and customs but also their beauty standards. This spread of Euro-centricism had profound effects that we still see today. In my practice, I often work with clients who struggle with beauty standards that were essentially imposed on their cultures generations ago.

* * *

I SEE this impact consistently in the work I do:

- Women who feel pressured to conform to European features
- People struggling with skin tone preferences rooted in colonial history
- Communities grappling with beauty standards that don't reflect their heritage

Understanding this history isn't about dwelling in the past; it's about making sense of our present struggles. When we recognize where these beauty standards came from, we can begin to question and challenge them.

> **Reflection Question:** *Think about the beauty standards you grew up with. Can you trace where they came from? How have they influenced your relationship with your body?*

This historical context helps us understand something crucial: beauty standards are created, not natural. They can be questioned, challenged, and changed. Knowing this can be incredibly liberating as we work to develop a healthier relationship with our bodies. As we continue through this chapter, we will unpack these ideas further.

Ancient Perspectives on Beauty

Standing in a museum one afternoon, I was captivated by Greek and Roman statues. These marble figures tell us so much about how different cultures have viewed the human body throughout time. In Ancient Greece and Rome, the ideal body represented more than appearance, it symbolized virtue, strength, and harmony.

The art from this period shows us bodies that were muscular and symmetrical. Think of the famous statues of Zeus or Hercules carved with incredible attention to physical detail. For women, the ideal emphasized athletic capability while maintaining feminine curves, suggesting both strength and grace.

But here's what's fascinating - while these artistic ideals existed, everyday life looked very different. Most people were focused on survival and daily work, not achieving a perfect physique. This gap between artistic ideals and reality isn't so different from what we experience today with social media and magazines.

What we can learn from this period is that beauty standards have always been more complex than they appear. While Greek and Roman art celebrated certain ideals, these weren't universal truths - they were cultural preferences of their time.

> **Reflection Question:** *How do today's artistic representations of bodies compare to these ancient ideals? What has changed, and what remains similar?*

The Renaissance: Celebrating Fullness

Imagine walking through a gallery of Renaissance paintings. You'd see something quite different from today's magazine covers bodies painted with curves, rounded bellies, and soft flesh. Artists like Peter Paul Rubens became famous for depicting figures that would be considered "plus size" by today's standards. During this period, a fuller figure often symbolized prosperity and health. This makes sense in historical context; in a time when food could be scarce, having enough to eat was a sign of wealth. These paintings remind us that what we consider "beautiful" is often tied to broader social and economic conditions.

However, this period also marked the beginning of significant changes in global beauty standards. As European influence spread worldwide, these Western ideals began to impact cultures that had their own unique and diverse standards of beauty. This shift continues to influence how we think about bodies today.

> **Reflection Exercise:** *Look at a Renaissance painting and a modern fashion magazine cover side by side. What differences do you notice? How do these differences make you feel about beauty standards today?*

The key insight here isn't just historical; it's about understanding that beauty standards are created by societies, not nature. They change over time and vary across cultures. This knowledge can be incredibly freeing as we work to develop healthy relationships with our bodies.

Cultural Practices and Body Politics: A Historical Lens on Beauty Standards

Throughout human civilization, societies have developed intricate systems to shape, control, and define the human body, particularly women's bodies. These practices weren't merely aesthetic choices; they represented complex webs of social control, cultural identity, and power dynamics. Like invisible threads weaving through society, these beauty standards bound individuals to specific roles and expectations.

Consider the Victorian corset; more than just a garment, it was society's iron grip on femininity. Women would endure the daily ritual of lacing themselves into these restrictive devices, often struggling to breathe properly, all in pursuit of the coveted hourglass figure. This wasn't simply about fashion; it was about molding women's bodies into physical manifestations of the period's rigid social expectations. The corset became a tangible symbol of how society literally shaped women to fit its ideals.

Across the globe, different cultures developed their own body-modifying practices, each reflecting unique social hierarchies and values. The Chinese practice of foot binding, for instance, transformed women's feet into tiny "golden lotuses," a painful tradition that simultaneously signified status and severely limited mobility. The Ndebele and Padaung communities' neck-lengthening practices, while celebrating cultural identity, also marked women's bodies as carriers of tradition and social standing.

When European colonization spread across continents, it didn't just bring political control; it carried with it Western beauty ideals that often clashed with indigenous standards. Imagine the profound disruption in societies where fuller figures were traditionally celebrated, suddenly facing pressure to conform to Victorian slenderness. Local practices that had evolved over centuries found themselves competing with imposed European standards, creating a complex hierarchy of beauty that often privileged Western ideals.

These historical practices remind us that beauty standards have never been neutral; they've always been instruments of social control, cultural expression, an,d sometimes, colonial power. Their legacy continues to influence modern beauty ideals, shaping how we view and value different body types today.

. . .

Reflection Questions: *Think about today's "invisible corsets";*

1. *What modern beauty practices restrict or reshape our bodies?*

Consider:

2. *High heels and their impact on posture and mobility*
3. *Shapewear and its modern parallel to historical corsetry*
4. *Cosmetic procedures and their relationship to social expectations*
5. *Diet culture and its grip on daily habits.*

How DO these practices continue to reflect power structures in society? Consider:

- Economic implications (cost of beauty treatments, gym memberships, etc.)
- Professional expectations around appearance
- Cultural and racial beauty standards
- Social media's role in reinforcing beauty norms

These beauty standards weren't created in a vacuum; they were carefully constructed and maintained through systems of power. Understanding this history helps us recognize why challenging these standards is so important and why representation matters so deeply in our ongoing journey toward true body acceptance.

The 20th Century: Beauty in Constant Motion

Sometimes, when I look at photographs from different decades of the 20th century, I'm struck by how dramatically beauty standards shifted. The 1920s brought us the flapper - rebellious, boyish, and corset-free. By the 1950s, everything had changed again, and curves were celebrated with icons like Marilyn Monroe. Each decade seemed to demand women transform themselves to fit new ideals.

In the 1980s and 1990s, the fashion industry saw the rise of supermodels, further reinforcing these beauty norms. Names like Cindy Crawford, Naomi Campbell, and Claudia Schiffer dominated runways and magazine covers. While Naomi Campbell broke some racial barriers, the industry was still primarily dominated by white women, perpetuating the thin, Eurocentric ideal. This era also saw the exoticization of non-white bodies, often reducing them to mere fashion statements rather than celebrating their intrinsic beauty. These supermodels were not just fashion icons; they became cultural symbols, influencing everything from makeup trends to fitness routines. The fashion industry's focus on thinness and specific facial features solidified a beauty standard that many women found impossible to attain, leading to widespread issues like body dysmorphia and eating disorders.

But beneath these changing fashions lay a deeper story about power and colonization through media. Hollywood and mass media became modern colonial forces, spreading Western beauty ideals globally. These images overwhelmingly featured white actresses with Eurocentric features, creating a narrow definition of beauty that excluded most of the world's women. For colonized and post-colonial societies, these images reinforced the racial hierarchies established during colonial rule, continuing to influence how people viewed themselves and others.

> **Reflection Exercise:** *Look at popular media from different decades of the 20th century. You can find this information in TIME magazine 100 Persons of the Century or the Media History Digital Library. Who was celebrated? Who was missing? How do these patterns still influence us today?*
>
> *Consider your early beauty icons. Who were they? How did they influence your perception of beauty? How do you see colonial influences in these standards?*

* * *

Colonialism's Shadow: The Intersection of Power, Class, and Beauty Standards

Imagine walking through a grand colonial mansion, its walls lined with portraits of the "ideal" beauty; European features, pale skin, slender frames. These weren't just paintings; they were powerful messages about who held social power and whose appearance was deemed "worthy." This is where our story of colonial beauty standards begins, and surprisingly, where many of our modern beauty ideals remain rooted.

The colonial project wasn't satisfied with merely claiming lands and resources, it sought to colonize minds and bodies too. European powers crafted a careful hierarchy of beauty that mirrored their political dominance. Like architects designing a social structure, they positioned their features; light skin, thinness, and European facial features, at the top of the beauty pyramid. Indigenous appearances weren't just different; they were systematically devalued, creating deep wounds in cultural identity that still haven't fully healed.

Think of class distinctions as the scaffolding that held these beauty standards in place. During industrialization, a thin body became a status symbol; a visible sign that you weren't doing manual labor. The wealthy could "afford" to be slim, creating a powerful association between thinness and social elevation. This wasn't just about looks; it was about power. Colonial authorities exported these class-based ideals, teaching colonized peoples that to be "civilized" meant adopting European standards of appearance.

The machinery of colonialism; schools, churches and media worked like a well-oiled beauty propaganda machine. Missionaries preached European ideals of "propriety" while schools taught children to value Western appearances. These weren't subtle suggestions; they were systematic attempts to reshape entire societies' understanding of beauty. The message was clear: to succeed in the colonial world, one had to literally embody colonial ideals.

Today, these colonial shadows linger in our beauty standards like persistent echoes.

In many former colonies, lighter skin and thinness are still highly valued and often seen as markers of beauty and success. The legacy of colonialism continues to influence media representation, fashion, and social norms. Skin-lightening products remain popular in many parts of the world, reflecting the deep-seated preference for lighter skin. Likewise, the fashion industry frequently prioritizes Western standards, marginalizing local aesthetics. These colonial influences continue to manifest in both subtle and overt ways. From beauty pageants to fashion magazines, we often witness the same limited standards being celebrated. But understanding this history gives us power. It helps us recognize that these standards weren't natural or inevitable they were constructed. And what has been constructed can be dismantled.

REFLECTION Questions

Personal Impact:
1. *How do you see colonial beauty standards influencing your own self-image?*
2. *What beauty practices in your culture might be traced back to colonial influence?*

Community Perspective:

    1. How does your community resist or reinforce
      colonial beauty standards?

    2. What local beauty traditions have survived despite
      colonial influence?

FUTURE CONSIDERATIONS:

- How can understanding this history help us create more inclusive beauty standards?
- What steps can we take to decolonize our personal beauty practices?

Feminism Meets Body Politics

I recently attended a conference where speakers discussed the evolution of feminist approaches to body image. Early feminist movements challenged beauty standards, but often from a limited perspective centered on white, Western experiences. While these early efforts were important, they missed crucial aspects of how beauty standards uniquely affect different communities. While it pushed back against the narrow confines of what society deemed attractive, it did not fully address the unique cultural pressures and racial biases that many women experience. As a result, the feminist discourse sometimes perpetuated a different set of exclusive standards, failing to resonate with a broader audience.

This is where intersectional feminism has made such a vital contribution. By recognizing how race, class, and other aspects of identity intersect with beauty standards, we've gained a deeper understanding of how colonial beauty norms affect different communities. Women of color often experience unique pressures regarding skin tone, hair texture, and facial features, which are directly linked to colonial beauty standards. The #BodyPositivity movement began celebrating diverse body types and non-Western ideals, highlighting beauty in various skin tones, hair textures, and body shapes. Alongside this, the concept of body neutrality has emerged, encouraging individuals to shift focus from appearance to appreciating what their bodies can do, fostering self-acceptance without the pressure to constantly feel positive about one's body. Together, these movements have been crucial in validating experiences that were previously marginalized or ignored, offering different but complementary paths to redefine our relationships with our bodies.

Despite growing awareness, colonial beauty norms persist through global media and marketing. But something powerful is happening: more voices are speaking up, challenging these standards, and celebrating diverse forms of beauty. Every time someone embraces their natural features or questions narrow beauty standards, they participate in this crucial transformation.

> **Reflection Moment:** *Think about your journey with beauty standards. How have different feminist perspectives shaped your understanding of beauty? What would true liberation from colonial beauty standards look like to you?*

Reflecting on Our Beauty Story

Last night, I sat looking through old family photographs spanning generations. Each image told a story about how beauty standards have shifted over time. I paused at a picture of my grandmother, remembering how she once told me about the beauty practices of her era, so different from today's; this moment reminded me how our understanding of beauty has always been in flux, shaped by forces larger than any individual.

Think of our collective beauty story as a river flowing through time. It begins in ancient civilizations, where Greek and Roman art celebrated muscular symmetry, then meanders through the Renaissance, where paintings honored fuller figures with soft curves. But this river took a sharp turn with European colonialism when Western beauty standards were forced upon diverse cultures worldwide. I think about how this impacts us even now - how many still struggle with internalized beliefs about light skin being "better" or certain features being more "desirable."

The 20th century added new currents to this river. Hollywood and mass media became powerful forces, broadcasting narrow beauty ideals globally. I remember watching old films and magazines and seeing how they celebrated primarily white, thin bodies as the epitome of beauty. Even as a professional in this field, I sometimes catch myself influenced by these deeply embedded standards. This is why understanding our beauty history matters, it helps us recognize that these standards weren't natural developments but constructed ideals that we can choose to challenge.

When I work with women today, I often share this historical perspective because it helps us understand that our struggles with body image are not just individual challenges but part of a larger story. Knowing this history doesn't immediately free us from its influence but gives us power. It helps us understand why we feel certain pressures and permits us to question these inherited standards.

As we move forward, we're part of a growing movement to redefine beauty on our own terms. Every time we celebrate diverse body types, challenge old standards, or support each other in self-acceptance, we're helping to write a new chapter in this ongoing story.

Our Complex Relationship with Media

As I scrolled through my social media feed this morning, I caught myself falling into a familiar pattern. Each perfectly curated image whispers messages about how I should look, what I should wear, and how to present myself to the world. It reminded me of a conversation with a friend who confessed she couldn't look at social media without feeling inadequate. I understood completely that we're all swimming in a sea of filtered perfection.

The media landscape we navigate today is more complex than ever before. It's not just magazines and television anymore; it's the constant stream of images on our phones, the influencers who seem to live picture-perfect lives, and the subtle and not-so-subtle messages about what bodies are worthy of being seen. I think about how different this experience is from even a generation ago when we at least had breaks from these messages. Now, they're with us everywhere, even in our bedrooms late at night as we scroll through our phones.

But what fascinates me most is how these beauty standards clash and merge across cultures. I remember visiting my friend's family in Hawaii, where their beauty ideals completely differed from what I grew up with. It was eye-opening to realize that what's considered "beautiful" in one culture might be completely different in another.

Yet, increasingly, Western beauty standards seep into every corner of the globe through our interconnected media.

Our families and communities add another layer to this story. The casual comments at family gatherings, the well-meaning but harmful advice from relatives, and the comparisons between siblings shape how we see ourselves just as powerfully as any magazine cover. I still remember my aunt's annual weight commentary at family reunions and how those words echoed in my mind long after the gatherings ended.

Yet, within this challenging landscape, I see hope. More people are questioning these standards, calling out unrealistic images, and creating spaces for celebrating diverse beauty. Every time someone shares an unfiltered photo or speaks honestly about their body image struggles, they create a crack in the perfect facade of toxic beauty culture.

* * *

Reflection Questions:

How does your social media consumption affect your body image? What changes might support your well-being?

What messages about beauty did you receive from your family and culture? How do these align or conflict with broader media messages?

Where do you find examples of authentic, diverse beauty in your daily life?

The Heart of Body Image

SITTING in my office one afternoon, I listened as a woman shared her daily ritual of body checking, constantly monitoring every perceived flaw, the mental catalog of every slight change in her appearance. Her story resonated with me, reflecting my own journey with body image and the significant psychological impact these concerns can have on our lives. The challenges, comparisons, and psychological toll are profound.

The weight of negative body image isn't just about appearance; it's about how we move through the world, connect with others, and allow ourselves to be seen and heard. I've witnessed how these struggles can ripple through every aspect of life, from avoiding social gatherings to holding back from professional opportunities. The internal dialogue can be exhausting: the constant self-criticism, the comparison to others, and the energy spent trying to shrink or modify ourselves to fit an impossible ideal.

I've learned, personally and professionally, that healing our relationship with our body isn't just about changing how we look; it's about changing how we think and feel. It's about recognizing when we're caught in cognitive distortions, those mental tricks that convince us our worth is tied to our appearance. I remember my own breakthrough moment when I realized how much of my negative self-talk was based on these distorted thoughts rather than reality.

The path to healing often begins with small steps. It might start with gentle movement that focuses on how our body feels rather than how it looks. It might begin with mindfulness practices that help us observe our thoughts without getting caught in their undertow. Sometimes, it's about finding supportive communities where we can share our struggles and celebrations without judgment.

What gives me hope is seeing how this healing ripples outward. When one person challenges their negative body image, they often inspire others to do the same. Every time we choose self-compassion over self-criticism, we create more space for others to do the same.

Reflection Questions:
*What would it feel like to spend a day focusing on how
your body feels rather than how it looks?*

How might your life be different if you could redirect the energy spent on body criticism toward things that truly matter to you?

What small step could you take today toward a more compassionate relationship with your body?

Who in your life supports your journey toward body acceptance, and how can you strengthen these connections?

Remember, this journey isn't linear, and that's okay. Some days will feel easier than others, but each step toward self-compassion is valuable, no matter how small it might seem.

Chapter 2

Embracing Diversity and Representation

"The only way to make a difference is to embrace and celebrate your body and all it does for you, regardless of what society says it should look like."
— **Ashley Graham**

The journey toward embracing diversity and representation is ongoing but vital. We can move toward a world where everybody is celebrated by recognizing the significance of seeing various body types in media and society, highlighting the benefits of diverse representation, acknowledging positive examples, and addressing challenges.

Last Saturday morning, I curled up in my favorite reading chair, a cup of tea growing cold beside me as I flipped through a fashion magazine. Page after page showed the same type of body: tall, slim, predominantly white models staring back at me. My heart felt heavy as I thought about Maria, a client I'd spoken with just days before, who tearfully shared how she'd never seen anyone who looked like her celebrated in media. I closed the magazine, remembering my own journey of searching for validation in those glossy pages, never quite finding myself there either.

There are often times I think about the countless conversations I've had with women in my practice, each sharing a similar story of feeling invisible in our media landscape. There was Sarah, who stopped wearing sleeveless tops because she never saw solid and muscular arms celebrated. Mei struggled with her Asian features because they didn't match the Western beauty standards that dominated her social media feed. These stories stay with me, reminding me why representation matters so profoundly.

The truth is, we're all searching for reflections of ourselves in the world around us. When we don't find them, something inside us questions our worth. I remember the first time I saw someone with my body type celebrated in a magazine; the surge of validation I felt was powerful enough to bring tears to my eyes. That moment helped me understand why diverse representation isn't just about checking boxes or meeting quotas; it's about acknowledging and celebrating the beautiful variety of human bodies that exist in our world.

Despite these positive steps, there are ongoing challenges to achieving true diversity in representation. Tokenism remains prevalent, where a single individual from a marginalized group is included to give the appearance of diversity without meaningful inclusion. Another hurdle is performative diversity, where brands or media outlets superficially embrace diversity without making systemic changes. Achieving real progress requires systemic change in industries like fashion and entertainment.

This means hiring diverse talent behind the scenes; designers, photographers, and executives who understand, value, and celebrate diverse body types. It also means creating workplace, educational, and (what other types?) policies and practices that promote genuine inclusivity.

As we begin this chapter, I want you to know that your unique body deserves to be seen and celebrated. Whether you've felt invisible in media representations or struggled to find role models who look like you, your story matters. Together, we'll explore why diverse representation is crucial, celebrate the progress we're seeing, and discuss how we can contribute to creating a more inclusive world.

Celebrating Every Body's Story

The other day, while organizing my closet, I came across a dress I'd kept from years ago. It was a size I thought I "should" be, hanging there like a reminder of all the times I'd tried to force my body to be something it wasn't. As I held that dress, I wondered how many of us keep these physical reminders of body standards that were never meant for us. That day, I finally donated the dress, and with it, one more "should" that had been weighing on my heart.

Bodies tell stories of survival, joy, and life lived fully. This makes me think of the stretch marks that map my journey through motherhood, the strong legs that carry me through my daily walks, and the arms that have held loved ones through both celebration and grief. Every body in this world carries its own unique narrative, written in skin, bone, fat, and muscle, each one worthy of celebration.

Sometimes, when walking down a busy street, I'll notice how beautifully different everyone is: tall, short, curvy, lean, muscular, and soft. It's like watching a living artwork of human diversity. Yet many of us have been taught to see these differences as flaws rather than the natural, gorgeous variation that makes our world rich and interesting. I remember one particularly powerful moment in a workshop I attended when a participant stood up and shared how she'd finally started wearing sleeveless tops after decades of hiding her arms. The room filled with tears and nods of recognition; so many of us are holding back from living fully because we've been told our bodies need to look a certain way.

The path to celebrating our bodies often begins with small steps. Maybe it's wearing that bright color you've been told "isn't flattering" (as if joy needs to be flattering!). It could be taking a photo without trying to hide behind others. For me, it started with buying clothes that fit my current body rather than waiting until I was "worthy" of new things. These might seem like simple actions, but they're radical acts of self-acceptance in a world that often tells us to shrink ourselves.

In this journey, I've witnessed the power of community. Something magical happens when we share our stories and celebrations with others who understand. The shame that thrives in isolation begins to dissolve in the light of shared experience. Whether in person or online, finding your people, those who celebrate bodies of all kinds can transform how you see yourself.

Reflection Questions:

What story does your body tell? What adventures, challenges, and triumphs has it carried you through?

Think of a time when you felt truly comfortable in your body. What made that moment special?

How might your life change if you treated your body as a trusted friend rather than something to fix?

What's one small way you could celebrate your body today just as it is?

Remember, celebrating our bodies isn't about forcing positivity every day - some days that feels impossible, and that's okay. It's about creating a gentler, more spacious way of living in our skin, making room for all the complex feelings while slowly building a foundation of respect and appreciation for the body that carries us through life.

Breaking Free from Media's Mirror

Last night, I caught myself in an all-too-familiar spiral. There I was, scrolling through social media before bed, each perfectly filtered image making me feel a little smaller, a little less worthy. Then I remembered something a wise friend once told me: "Social media is like a highlight reel of everyone's best moments, filtered through their most flattering lens." I put down my phone and looked in my bedroom mirror, seeing not the "flaws" social media had trained me to focus on but a face that had smiled through countless joys and weathered many storms.

The relationship between media and our self-image runs deep. I think about the teenagers who come to my workshops, their phones filled with apps that automatically smooth their skin and slim their bodies. One young woman shared how she no longer knew what she really looked like without filters. Her words haunted me because I understood that feeling - that disconnect between our real selves and the images we're told we should aspire to be.

But here's what gives me hope: I'm witnessing a shift in how we consume and create media. More people are pulling back the curtain, showing the reality behind the perfect posts. I remember the first time I saw a popular influencer post-side-by-side photos - one carefully posed and filtered, the other natural and relaxed. It felt like someone had finally given us permission to be real.

The key isn't to completely avoid media, that's nearly impossible in today's world. Instead, it's about becoming more conscious consumers. Think of it like being a detective, investigating the stories behind the images we see. When I scroll through my feed now, I ask myself: "What's the message behind this image? How is it making me feel? Is this contributing to my well-being or diminishing it?"

I've learned to curate my media diet as carefully as I do my food choices. Just as we nourish our bodies with healthy food, we need to feed our minds with content that uplifts and empowers us. This might mean unfollowing accounts that trigger comparison, seeking out diverse representations of beauty, or limiting social media time altogether.

The most powerful moment often comes when we start creating our own media narrative. Rosa, started sharing unfiltered photos of her workout journey, not to showcase a "perfect" body but to celebrate what her body could do. Her courage inspired others to do the same, creating a ripple effect of authenticity in her community.

Reflection Questions:

*How does your current media consumption make you
    feel about your body?*
*What would change if you followed accounts that
    celebrated bodies like yours?*
*Can you identify three ways to make your social media
    feed more body-positive?*
*What message would you like to share with others
    about real beauty?*

MEDIA AWARENESS EXERCISE:

Take a day to notice your media consumption patterns. Each time you look at social media or other media, jot down:

- What you're looking at
- How it makes you feel
- Whether it adds to or diminishes your self-worth

At the end of the day, review your notes. What patterns do you notice? What changes might support your well-being?

Remember, changing our relationship with media isn't about perfection but progress. Some days, we'll get caught in the comparison trap, and that's okay. What matters is that we keep learning, growing, and choosing content that reflects the diverse, beautiful reality of human bodies.

A World of Beautiful Bodies

In many parts of the world, body positivity takes on unique cultural flavors, reflecting the values and traditions of different societies. For instance, in some African cultures, fuller bodies are often celebrated as symbols of wealth, health, and fertility. Traditional dances and ceremonies frequently showcase and honor these body types, reinforcing a positive body image within the community. Similarly, in Polynesian cultures, larger bodies are often associated with strength and beauty. Hula dancing, for example, celebrates bodies of all shapes and sizes, focusing on grace and storytelling rather than conforming to a specific body standard.

These cultural norms and values play a significant role in promoting body positivity. They offer a broader perspective on beauty, including diverse body types. By embracing these cultural practices, you can see that beauty is not confined to a single standard but is as varied as the people who inhabit this world. Learning about these practices can help you appreciate your body more and see the beauty in others. For example, Japanese culture often emphasizes harmony and balance, which includes accepting one's natural body shape. This cultural perspective can be incredibly liberating, allowing you to focus on well-being rather than appearance.

Personal narratives from different cultural contexts provide powerful testimonies of body positivity. Consider the story of Aisha from Nigeria, who grew up in a community that celebrated fuller figures. Despite being exposed to Western beauty standards through media, Aisha found confidence in her body by participating in local dance traditions that honored her natural shape. Another inspiring story is that of Mei in China, who struggled with societal pressure to be thin. Mei found solace in traditional Tai Chi practices emphasizing inner peace and physical health over appearance. These stories highlight how cultural practices can offer a refuge from the pressures of mainstream beauty standards.

However, the journey to body acceptance is not without its challenges. Navigating societal expectations can be incredibly difficult in cultures with rigid body standards. In South Korea, for example, where societal beauty standards are particularly rigid, cosmetic surgery has become a widespread practice, with many individuals turning to procedures like double eyelid surgery to align with the culturally valued ideal of beauty. This cultural expectation can lead to intense scrutiny and criticism, making it challenging for individuals to embrace their natural bodies. The impact of these cultural expectations can be profound, affecting mental health and self-esteem. Strategies for navigating these norms include seeking out supportive communities and engaging in practices prioritizing well-being over appearance. For instance, joining a group that promotes body positivity or practicing self-compassion exercises can provide much-needed support.

Understanding and appreciating different cultural perspectives on body image can significantly enhance body positivity. Cultural humility and openness are crucial in this process. By learning from other cultures, you can gain insights that challenge your preconceived notions of beauty. This broader perspective can help you develop a more inclusive and accepting view of your body. For example, adopting practices such as mindfulness from Buddhist traditions can help you cultivate a more compassionate relationship with your body. Additionally, engaging with cultural narratives and traditions celebrating body diversity can provide new ways to appreciate and honor your body.

By embracing these diverse perspectives, you enrich your

understanding and contribute to a more inclusive society. When you appreciate beauty in all its forms, you help dismantle the narrow standards that have long dictated what is considered attractive. This shift in perspective is not just beneficial for you; it has a ripple effect, influencing those around you to embrace a more inclusive view of beauty. By promoting cross-cultural understanding and empathy, you play a part in creating a world where everybody is celebrated.

Understanding how different cultures approach body positivity and diversity offers a rich tapestry of perspectives that can inspire and uplift. By embracing these diverse narratives and practices, you can find new ways to appreciate your own body and those of others. This inclusive approach enhances self-esteem and promotes a more accepting and compassionate society. As we move forward, we will explore how to integrate these insights into practical steps for fostering self-acceptance and breaking free from diet culture.

The aroma of incense and the sound of traditional drums filled the air at a cultural festival I attended last summer. As I watched dancers of all shapes and sizes move with grace and confidence, I was struck by how differently beauty is celebrated across cultures. One performer, her body strong and curved, moved with such joy and pride that the audience couldn't help but be moved. It reminded me how narrow our Western beauty standards can be and how much we miss when we limit ourselves to a single definition of beauty.

My friend Amara, shared stories of growing up in West Africa, where her fuller figure was celebrated as a sign of prosperity and health. "In my grandmother's village," she told me, "they would worry if someone was too thin. Beauty meant having enough curves to dance properly!" Her laughter was infectious as she demonstrated the traditional movements that celebrated rather than shamed her body. Through her stories, I began to see how cultural perspectives can heal or harm our relationship with our bodies.

The wisdom of different cultures offers us so many beautiful alternatives to the restrictive beauty standards many of us grew up with. In Japan, the concept of "wabi-sabi" celebrates the beauty of imperfection and natural aging. Traditional Polynesian dance honors the power and grace of all body types. These aren't just interesting cultural facts but invitations to see our bodies through different, more compassionate lenses.

Yet, I also recognize the complexity of navigating multiple cultural beauty standards. Min-Ji, shared her struggle to balance her Korean heritage's emphasis on slenderness with her growing appreciation for body acceptance. "Some days," she told me, "I feel caught between worlds." Her journey reminds us that cultural body standards can uplift and challenge us, sometimes simultaneously.

From these diverse perspectives, I've learned that beauty is not a single story but a tapestry of countless narratives. Each culture contributes its own thread, creating a richer, more inclusive picture of what it means to have and celebrate a body. When we open ourselves to these different viewpoints, we often find new ways to appreciate our own bodies.

Reflection Questions:

*What beauty standards did your culture of origin
   teach you about bodies?*

*How have other cultural perspectives influenced your
   view of beauty?*

*What cultural practices or traditions help you feel
   more connected to your body?*

*What would it be if you could adopt one body-positive
   aspect from another culture?*

Cultural Connection Exercise:

Take a moment to explore a cultural tradition that celebrates bodies differently from what you're used to. This might mean:

- Watching traditional dance performances
- Learning about beauty rituals from different cultures

- Reading stories about body image from various cultural perspectives
- Trying movement practices from other traditions

Remember, exploring other cultural perspectives isn't about appropriation; it's about opening our minds to different ways of seeing and celebrating bodies. Each culture's wisdom can help us build a more inclusive and compassionate understanding of human beauty.

As we embrace these diverse perspectives, we create space for everybody to feel seen and celebrated. Whether discovering the joy of traditional dance, finding peace in ancient mindfulness practices, or simply learning to see beauty through a different cultural lens, each step toward understanding enriches our collective journey toward body acceptance.

Chapter 3

Cultivating Self-Acceptance

"Loving yourself isn't vanity. It's sanity"— **Katrina Mayer**

One quiet morning, I wandered into a cozy independent bookstore, the smell of paper and ink filling the air. I found myself lingering near the memoir section when I noticed two women standing nearby, engrossed in conversation. One woman, clutching a book about body positivity, spoke softly about her ongoing struggle to accept herself as she is. Holding a book on mindfulness, the other nodded sympathetically, sharing how years of internalized criticism had shaped her self-image. As I listened, I realized how universal these experiences are, whether spoken aloud or kept hidden. This chapter is dedicated to uncovering the roots of that internal dialogue and providing tools to transform it into a more compassionate and empowering narrative.

The journey toward self-acceptance often feels like trying to swim upstream. I remember my own turning point, sitting cross-legged on my office floor after a long day of counseling sessions, surrounded by sticky notes covered in positive affirmations that felt impossible to believe. That moment taught me something crucial:

self-acceptance isn't about forcing positivity; it's about creating space for all our feelings while gradually building a foundation of self-compassion.

At the heart of all healing lies self-acceptance, it's the soil from which every positive change grows. What I've learned, both personally and through working with countless women, is that self-acceptance isn't a destination we reach once, but rather like tending a garden that needs daily care. Some days, we plant seeds of kindness; other days, we gently pull out weeds of self-doubt. There are seasons of vibrant growth and quiet seasons of rest, each playing its vital role in our healing journey. When we finally embrace all parts of ourselves, our strengths and struggles, our victories and vulnerabilities, we create a foundation of inner peace that no external validation can shake. This gentle self-embrace creates the sacred space where our wounds can heal, where our spirit can breathe, and where transformation naturally unfolds. What matters isn't perfection but our willingness to keep showing up, to keep nurturing this relationship with ourselves, knowing that each small act of self-acceptance is a step toward deeper healing. Like a garden that blooms in its own time, our journey of self-acceptance creates the perfect conditions for healing to flourish.

What I've learned, both personally and through working with others, is that self-acceptance is less like a destination and more like tending a garden. Some days, we plant seeds of kindness; other days, we pull out weeds of self-doubt. There are seasons of growth and seasons of rest. What matters isn't perfection but our willingness to keep showing up, to keep nurturing this relationship with ourselves.

In this chapter, we'll explore practical tools for cultivating self-acceptance, understanding the difference between acceptance and resignation, and learning how to navigate the challenging days when self-love feels out of reach. We'll discuss how to handle the well-meaning but sometimes harmful messages from family and friends, and how to build a support system that nurtures our growth.

· · ·

Reflection Moment:

*Before we begin this journey together, take a quiet
   moment to consider:*

What does self-acceptance mean to you?

*What messages about your worth would you like to
   challenge?*

*What small step toward self-acceptance feels possible
   today?*

Who or what supports you in this journey?

REMEMBER, wherever you are in your journey toward self-acceptance is exactly where you need to be right now. Let's walk this path together, with gentleness and understanding for ourselves and each other.

Befriending Our Inner Voice

Last week, as I stood in front of my bathroom mirror getting ready for work, I caught myself in a familiar pattern. "You look tired... you should try harder... why can't you just..." The voice was so automatic I almost didn't notice it. Then I paused, remembering how many of us start our days this way, our inner critics already working overtime before we've even finished our morning coffee.

That harsh inner voice, we all know it well. It's the one that whispers "not good enough" when we're trying our best, or "you'll never manage this" when we're facing challenges. Emma, shared in a workshop how she'd spent years believing her negative thoughts were just "being realistic." It wasn't until she started writing them down that she realized how unkind, and often untrue, these thoughts really were.

The science behind negative self-talk is fascinating. These thought patterns aren't random; they're often deeply grooved pathways in our minds, carved by years of experiences, cultural messages, and learned behaviors. Understanding these patterns can be incredibly freeing; these thoughts aren't facts, they're habits. And like any habit, they can be transformed with patience and practice.

Let me share a technique that's been transformative for many people I've worked with. We call it the "Best Friend Test." When a negative thought arises, ask yourself: "Would I say this to my dearest friend?" Usually, the answer is a resounding no. This simple question can help us catch those harsh thoughts and begin to shift them toward something more compassionate.

Here's what this might look like in practice:

NEGATIVE THOUGHT —————————— **Pause and Reframe**

"I hate how I look."——— Who taught me to feel this way about my body? Whose standards am I trying to meet

I'm too big/small/tall/short———— My body is uniquely mine, and that's exactly as it should be."

"Everyone else looks better than me," ——-"Everybody tells a different story, and mine is still being written."

"I need to fix my body"————"What if my body isn't a problem to be solved but a partner to be appreciated?"

"I'm terrible at this,"————"I'm learning something new, and

that takes time."

"I'll never get better," —————"I'm taking steps forward, even if they're small."

"I'm not good enough"—————"Good enough for what? According to whom?"

* * *

MINDFULNESS PLAYS a crucial role in this work. Imagine your mind as a clear mountain lake, sometimes rippled by thoughts but capable of profound stillness. This is the essence of mindfulness, a practice that invites us to fully inhabit each moment of our lives with gentle awareness. Like a compassionate observer, mindfulness teaches us to witness our thoughts, emotions, and bodily sensations without becoming entangled in them. Rather than fighting against our experiences or getting lost in past regrets and future worries, we learn to stand firmly in the present moment. Think of it as developing a gentle observer within yourself who can notice these thoughts without getting swept away by them. Try this simple practice: For just one minute, close your eyes and notice your thoughts as if they're clouds passing in the sky. There is no need to chase them or push them away; just observe them floating by.

The goal isn't to never have negative thoughts; that's not realistic or even helpful. Instead, we're learning to create space between ourselves and these thoughts, to respond rather than react. As one client beautifully put it, "I'm learning to be the weather, not the storm."

Daily Practice Suggestions:

- Keep a small notebook handy to jot down negative thoughts as they arise.
- Practice the "Best Friend Test" when you catch critical self-talk.

- Take three deep breaths before responding to negative thoughts.
- Write a compassionate letter to yourself about a current struggle.

Reflection Questions:
What is your most common form of negative self-talk?
When do you notice it appears most strongly?
*What would change if you spoke to yourself as kindly
as you speak to those you love?*
*What small step could you take today toward more
self-compassionate dialogue?*

Remember, transforming our inner dialogue isn't about forcing positivity but cultivating a kinder, more understanding relationship with ourselves. Some days, this will feel easier than others, and that's perfectly okay. What matters is our willingness to keep showing up for ourselves, one gentle thought at a time.

Weaving Self-Compassion Into Every Day

As I poured my first cup of coffee this morning, I noticed the gentle morning light streaming through my kitchen window. Instead of rushing to check my phone or make a to-do list, I simply took a moment to be present. These small moments, I've learned, are where self-compassion often begins, not in grand gestures but in quiet acts of kindness toward ourselves.

Creating a daily practice of self-compassion is like tending a garden. We plant seeds of kindness through morning gratitude, water them with gentle movement, and watch them grow through consistent care. I remember the day I started my first gratitude journal. It felt awkward at first, searching for things to appreciate about myself. But like any new habit, it grew easier with time. That morning ritual of writing three things I'm grateful for feels as natural as breathing.

Let me share something that transformed my own practice: creating a sanctuary space. I've arranged a comfortable chair, a soft blanket, and a small table holding my journal and favorite pen in the corner of my bedroom. This isn't just a physical space; it's a promise to myself, a reminder that I deserve moments of peace and self-reflection. One of my clients called her similar space her "compassion corner," where she retreats for five minutes of mindful breathing when the world feels too heavy.

Movement becomes medicine when we approach it with compassion. Gone are the days of punishing exercise routines, or exercise purely to burn off those "extra calories." Instead, imagine greeting your body each morning like an old friend. It could be gentle stretches while the kettle boils or a mindful walk where you notice the feeling of earth beneath your feet. One woman in my practice discovered joy in dancing alone in her living room – no rules, no judgment, just pure celebration of movement.

The language we use with ourselves matters deeply. I often suggest creating a "Compassion Phrase Bank," a collection of gentle responses to difficult moments.

For instance:
Instead of "I should be better at this by now,"
Try "I'm exactly where I need to be in my journey."
When we stumble or struggle, these phrases become soft landing places for our hearts.

Daily Compassion Practices:

- Morning Moments: Start with three breaths and three gratitudes.
- Body Blessing: Thank your body for one thing it does for you each day.

- Evening Reflection: Write down one way you showed yourself kindness.
- Sanctuary Space: Create your own space for peaceful moments and spend some time there every day.

Reflection Questions:

What small act of self-kindness could you add to your morning routine?

Where in your home could you create a sanctuary space?

What phrase would you like to offer yourself during challenging moments?

How might your day feel different if you approached it with gentle awareness?

Remember, self-compassion isn't about being perfect; it's about being present with ourselves in all our beautiful complexity. Some days it might look like meditation and journaling; other days, it might simply be remembering to breathe deeply while waiting in traffic. What matters is the intention to treat ourselves with the same kindness we'd offer a dear friend.

As you move through your days, try to catch moments where you can pause and offer yourself a breath of compassion. These small acts of kindness toward ourselves ripple outward, transforming not only our inner landscape but our interactions with the world around us.

* * *

3.3 The Power of Speaking Life to Ourselves

Last evening, while cleaning out my desk drawer, I found an old notebook. Inside were affirmations I'd written years ago, each one a gentle rebellion against the self-doubt that had followed me for so long. Some made me smile, others brought tears to my eyes, but all reminded me of an important truth: **the words we speak to ourselves have power.** They can either be seeds that grow into gardens of self-belief or weeds that choke our confidence.

The science behind affirmations fascinates me. Our brains are like sophisticated recording devices that play back what we repeatedly tell them. Through neuroplasticity, our brain's remarkable ability to form new pathways allows us to rewire our thought patterns. Sarah, shared her story in one of my workshops about how after years of looking in the mirror and seeing only flaws, she began saying daily, "I appreciate my body's strength and resilience." At first, the words felt foreign, almost false. But gradually, like water-wearing away stone, these new thoughts began to create paths through her old patterns of self-criticism.

Creating personal affirmations is like writing love letters to ourselves. Generic phrases often fall flat because they don't speak to our unique experiences and struggles. I remember working with a client who transformed "I am beautiful" (which felt impossible for her to believe) into "I honor my body's journey and all it has carried me through." This subtle shift made the affirmation feel true and powerful for her.

Affirmations can be a powerful tool for building a positive self-image. You can harness their full potential by understanding their psychological basis, creating personalized affirmations, integrating them into your daily routine, and using visualization techniques. These practices can help cultivate a more positive and empowering mindset, enhancing your overall well-being and self-acceptance.

Let me share some practical ways to weave affirmations into your daily life:

- Morning Mirror Moment: Place a positive phrase on your bathroom mirror.
- Phone Reminders: Set affirmations as your phone's lock screen.
- Voice Notes: Record affirmations in your own voice to play during your commute,before an important meeting, or before any other situation in which your inner critic tends to speak loudly.
- Journaling: Write your chosen affirmation three times each morning.

Visualization techniques can further enhance the effectiveness of affirmations.

Visualization involves creating a mental image of your affirmation as if it's already true. For example, if your affirmation is "I am confident and successful," visualize yourself in a situation where you feel this way. Imagine the sights, sounds, and feelings associated with this scenario. This mental rehearsal can make your affirmations feel more natural and achievable. Creating a vision board is another powerful visualization tool. Gather images, quotes, and words that represent your affirmations and goals. Arrange them on a board and place them somewhere you'll see them daily. This visual representation can constantly remind you of your aspirations, keeping you motivated and focused.

Visualization Exercise: Creating a Vision Board

Take some time to gather materials for your vision board. Look for magazines and printouts, or even draw images that resonate with your affirmations and goals. Arrange these items on a board, adding quotes or words that inspire you. Place your vision board where you'll see it daily, such as in your bedroom or office. Spend a few minutes each day looking at your vision board, visualizing yourself achieving these goals and embodying these affirmations. This exercise can help solidify your affirmations in your mind, making them feel more tangible and attainable.

Visualization adds another layer of power to these practices. When I work with clients, I often suggest they create a "Future Memory." Close your eyes and imagine yourself already embodying your affirmation. Feel it in your body. What does confidence feel like on your shoulders? How does self-acceptance show in your smile? This mental rehearsal helps bridge the gap between aspiration and reality.

· · ·

CREATING YOUR PERSONAL AFFIRMATIONS:
1. Identify areas where you seek growth
2. Transform challenges into positive statements
3. Make them specific and personal
4. Write them in present tense
5. Include how they make you feel

Reflection Questions:
What words do you most need to hear right now?
Which area of your life could benefit from positive affirmations?
How might your day change if you started it with self-affirming words?
What's one affirmation you could create that feels authentic to you?

Find a quiet moment and comfortable space. Close your eyes and imagine yourself six months from now, feeling confident and at peace. What do you see? How do you carry yourself? What thoughts run through your mind? Let this vision guide you in creating affirmations that bridge the gap between now and then.

Remember, affirmations aren't about denying reality or forcing positivity. They're about planting seeds of possibility, nurturing new ways of seeing ourselves. Some days they'll feel more true than others, and that's okay. What matters is the consistent practice of speaking kindness to ourselves, even, especially, when it feels challenging.

The journey of transforming our self-talk is both tender and powerful. Each affirmation we speak is like a small act of courage, a step toward believing in our inherent worth. Let's take these steps together, one affirming word at a time.

3.4 Finding Beauty in Our Perfectly Imperfect Selves

When I was younger, I often found myself fixated on my imperfections, believing they were flaws that needed to be hidden or fixed. However, as I grew older and gained more experience, I realized that these so-called imperfections were simply part of being human. They were not flaws but unique aspects that made me who I am. Embracing your imperfections is the first step toward self-acceptance. Start by acknowledging them without judgment. A powerful exercise is to write down a list of your perceived imperfections. Be honest with yourself and include everything that comes to mind, no matter how trivial it may seem. Once you have your list, take a moment to reflect on each item. Consider how these imperfections have shaped you and what you have learned from them. This exercise helps you view your imperfections as valuable parts of your identity rather than flaws to be hidden.

Many well-known figures have publicly embraced their imperfections, serving as powerful examples of self-acceptance. For instance, actress Kate Winslet has spoken openly about her body image struggles and her decision to embrace her natural look, including her curves and wrinkles. Similarly, singer and actress Demi Lovato has been vocal about her battles with body dysmorphia and eating disorders, choosing to celebrate her body as it is. These stories remind us that even those in the public eye, who often face immense pressure to appear perfect, have their struggles and have found strength in embracing their imperfections. Their journeys can serve as inspiration for you to do the same.

Shifting your focus from perfection to progress is a crucial mindset change. Perfection is an unattainable goal that can lead to constant disappointment and frustration. Instead, try to value progress and growth. Set realistic and attainable goals and celebrate the small victories along the way. For example, if you aim to improve your fitness, acknowledge your progress each week, whether running a little farther or lifting slightly heavier weights. These small milestones are significant and deserve recognition. Celebrating your progress, no matter how minor it may seem, helps reinforce a positive mindset and encourages you to keep moving forward.

Cultivating a growth mindset can further support your journey to self-acceptance. Psychologist Carol Dweck developed the concept of a growth mindset, which asserts that people can develop their abilities and intelligence through effort and practice. In contrast, a fixed mindset views abilities as static and unchangeable. Embracing a growth mindset involves recognizing that challenges and setbacks are opportunities for learning and growth rather than reflections of your inherent worth. For instance, if you face a setback at work, instead of thinking, "I'm not good at this," reframe it to, "This is a chance for me to learn and improve." Growth mindset affirmations, such as "I am capable of learning new things" and "Every challenge is an opportunity to grow," can reinforce this mindset and help you approach life with a more positive and resilient attitude.

Practicing forgiveness and self-compassion is essential for self-acceptance. We all make mistakes, and holding onto guilt or resentment can hinder our ability to move forward. Learning to forgive yourself for past mistakes is a powerful act of self-love. One effective exercise is to write a forgiveness letter to yourself. In this letter, acknowledge your mistakes, express understanding and compassion for yourself, and offer forgiveness. This exercise can help release the emotional weight of past mistakes and create space for healing and growth.

Self-compassion meditations can also support this process. These meditations involve focusing on feelings of compassion and kindness towards yourself, especially during times of suffering or failure. Regularly practicing self-compassion can cultivate a more forgiving and nurturing relationship with yourself. Kristen Neff, a leading researcher in the field of self-compassion, emphasizes the importance of treating oneself with the same kindness and understanding that one would offer to a close friend in times of struggle. Her work has significantly contributed to the development of Mindful Self-Compassion (MSC), a practice designed to help individuals reduce self-criticism and increase emotional resilience. You can explore more about Kristen Neff and her work on her website: https://self-compassion.org.

Embracing your imperfections, valuing progress over perfection, cultivating a growth mindset, and practicing forgiveness and self-compassion are all integral steps toward self-acceptance. These practices help you see yourself in a more positive and loving light, recognizing that you are worthy and deserving of kindness just as you are. As you continue to integrate these practices into your life, you will find that self-acceptance becomes a natural and empowering part of your journey. Next, we will explore practical strategies for integrating intuitive eating into your daily routine, helping you build a healthier and more positive relationship with food.

The other day, while sorting through old photographs, I came across one that made me pause. It was a picture I'd once hidden away because I thought my smile was too wide, my laugh lines too visible. Now, years later, I found myself touched by the joy captured in that moment, those very "imperfections" I'd once criticized now seemed to hold the essence of who I am.

This journey of embracing our imperfections isn't always easy. Countless conversations come to mind with women who speak of their perceived flaws as if they're apologies they owe the world. One remarkable woman shared how she'd spent years hiding her vitiligo until her young daughter asked why she was trying to cover up her "beautiful butterfly patterns." That moment transformed how she saw herself, what she'd viewed as a flaw became a mark of uniqueness.

The media often celebrates stories of public figures embracing their authenticity. Kate Winslet's powerful stance against digital editing and Demi Lovato's raw honesty about their struggles have helped crack the veneer of perfection we're often pressured to maintain. But the most profound stories I've witnessed have been quieter ones – the woman who finally stopped dyeing her gray hair and felt truly herself for the first time in years, or the dancer who learned to celebrate her strong, muscular legs that didn't fit the traditional ballet mold.

Shifting from perfection to progress feels like exhaling after holding your breath for too long. Instead of aiming for an impossible ideal, we can celebrate the small victories: the courage to wear that sleeveless top, the ability to look in the mirror with kindness, the strength to say "no" to crash diets. These aren't just steps forward; they're revolutionary acts of self-acceptance.

Dr. Carol Dweck's research on growth mindset offers us a powerful framework for this journey. When we view our challenges as opportunities for growth rather than evidence of our inadequacy, everything shifts. I remember working with an artist who transformed her self-criticism about her technical skills into curiosity about what she could learn her art flourished when she stopped demanding perfection from herself.

Gentle Practices for Embracing Imperfection:

- Start an "I'm Proud Of" journal, celebrating small victories.
- Practice the "Mirror Moment" – find one thing you appreciate about yourself each morning.
- Create a self-forgiveness ritual for when you're being hard on yourself.
- Collect "Evidence of Growth" – noting how far you've come rather than how far you think you need to go.

Reflection Questions:
What "imperfection" might actually be one of your unique strengths?
How would you treat your perceived flaws if you viewed them through the eyes of someone who loves you?

What small step could you take today toward
accepting a part of yourself you usually criticize?
How might your life change if you redirected the
energy spent pursuing perfection toward pursuing
growth?

Remember, self-acceptance isn't about reaching a destination of perfect self-love. It's about creating a gentler relationship with ourselves, one that makes room for both our strengths and our struggles. Some days this will feel easier than others, and that's perfectly okay. What matters is that we keep showing up for ourselves, embracing all the perfectly imperfect pieces that make us who we are.

As we close this chapter, I invite you to take a moment to acknowledge how far you've come. Every step toward self-acceptance, no matter how small it might seem, is significant. You're not just changing your relationship with yourself; you're contributing to a world where authenticity and self-acceptance become the norm rather than the exception.

Chapter 4

When Body and Mind Dance Together

"We need to reshape our own perception of how we view ourselves. We have to step up as women and take the lead."
— **Beyoncé**

One evening, as the sun began to set, it cast long shadows across my living room floor. I did what so many of us do: scroll through social media. A post stopped my thumb mid-scroll. A woman had shared her raw, honest struggle with body image and anxiety, her words reaching through the screen and touching something deep within me. "Some days," she wrote, "I feel like I'm at war with my own reflection, and the battlefield extends into every corner of my mind."

Her vulnerability cracked open a space for memory, and I found myself remembering countless similar conversations in my office, over coffee with friends, in support groups where women shared this same intricate dance between body anxiety and mental health. I thought about Linda, who described her anxiety as a lens that magnified every perceived flaw, and Maria, whose panic attacks often began with catching an unexpected glimpse of herself in a store window.

The connection between our body image and mental health

runs deep, like the roots of the same tree intertwining beneath the surface. When we struggle with one, the other often follows suit, creating a cycle that can feel impossible to break. Yet understanding this connection is usually the first step toward healing both.

In this chapter, we'll explore the delicate relationship between our mental health and how we see ourselves. We'll look at practical tools for managing anxiety, depression, and other mental health challenges that often accompany body image struggles. More importantly, we'll discuss how to create a gentler, more compassionate approach to our bodies and minds.

Reflection Moment:

How does your mental health affect how you see your body?

How does your body image change when you're feeling anxious or low?

What helps you feel more grounded in both body and mind?

What would it mean to treat both your mental health and body image with equal compassion?

REMEMBER, you're not alone in this experience. The path to healing often begins with acknowledging these connections and understanding that caring for our minds and bodies isn't two separate journeys; they're part of the same path toward wholeness.

4.1 When Anxiety and Body Image Collide

Last week, I found myself frozen in a department store fitting room, my heart racing as I caught my reflection in the three-way mirror. The familiar wave of anxiety washed over me – the kind that makes your chest tight and your thoughts spiral. At that moment, I remembered all the women who've sat across from me, describing this exact experience: the way anxiety and body image concerns weave together like two strands of the same rope, each pulling tighter on the other.

Think of anxiety and body image as dance partners, moving in perfect, if painful, synchronization. When one leads, the other follows. I remember Anna, who shared how her anxiety would spike before social events, not because of the social interaction itself, but because of the overwhelming fear of being judged for her appearance. Her story echoes a truth many of us know too well – how society's unrealistic standards can turn every mirror into a potential trigger, every social gathering into an exercise in self-consciousness.

Our bodies speak the language of anxiety in ways we might not always recognize. Sometimes, it's the racing heart when trying on clothes or the sweaty palms before a beach day. Other times, it's more subtle, such as the constant mirror checking that becomes a security blanket or the elaborate routines we create to feel "presentable enough" to face the world. Maya, would spend hours getting ready, not out of joy but out of fear, each minute was an attempt to control the uncontrollable.

But here's what I've learned, personally and professionally: we can learn to quiet these anxious thoughts about our bodies. It's like learning a new language, the language of self-compassion and presence. Let me share some gentle practices that have helped many women find their way back to peace:

The Anxiety-Ease Toolkit:

- Breath Anchoring: When anxiety rises, place one hand on your heart, the other on your belly. Breathe deeply, feeling the rise and fall. This reminds us that our bodies are allies, not enemies.
- Body Scanning with Kindness: Starting at your toes and moving up, notice each part of your body without judgment. Thank each part for what it does for you.

- Present-moment grounding: When anxious thoughts about your body arise, touch something with an interesting texture. Focus on how it feels against your skin. This will bring you back to the now.

I remember Emma's transformation, how she went from avoiding social situations to gradually finding peace with her reflection. She started small, with just three deep breaths, whenever anxiety struck. Over time, she added more tools to her comfort kit: supportive self-talk, gentle movement, and reaching out to friends who understood. Her journey reminds us that healing is possible, one conscious breath at a time.

Reflection Questions:
*When does body-related anxiety feel strongest
for you?
What helps you feel most grounded when anxiety
rises?
How might your relationship with your body change if
anxiety weren't in the picture?
What small step could you take today toward
befriending your anxious body?*

Daily Practice Suggestion:
Create your anxiety-ease plan. Write down:
1. Three situations that typically trigger body anxiety
2. Two grounding techniques that feel accessible to you
3. One person you can reach out to for support
4. A gentle reminder to yourself for difficult moments

REMEMBER, managing anxiety about our bodies isn't about eliminating all negative thoughts – it's about creating space between the thought and our response. It's about learning to hold ourselves with gentleness when anxiety rises, knowing that both the anxiety and the moment will pass.

Your body and mind are not enemies to be conquered but allies to be understood. Each step toward managing anxiety, no matter how small, is a step toward a more peaceful relationship with your body.

4.2 When the Mirror Feeds the Darkness

Yesterday, I received an email from a woman who described her experience with depression and body image in a way that stopped me in my tracks. "Some days," she wrote, "it feels like my reflection and my mood are having a conversation I'm not invited to, but one that determines how my entire day will unfold." Her words captured something I've witnessed countless times: the profound connection between how we see our bodies and the weight of depression.

Think of depression and negative body image as shadows that often grow darker together. I remember sitting with Jamie, who described how her depression would color everything about her appearance darker, heavier, and worse. On days when the depression felt strongest, her reflection became an enemy, each glimpse in the mirror reinforcing the heavy feelings that already filled her heart.

The signs of this dance between depression and body image can be subtle yet profound. Sometimes, it shows up as the inability to feel joy in activities that once brought pleasure, like avoiding the beach you once loved or the dance class that used to light you up. Other times, the quiet voice turns every mirror into a judgment zone, every photograph into evidence of perceived inadequacy.

LET me share what I've learned about navigating these waters:
Daily Comfort Practices:

- Morning self-check-in: How does your heart feel today?
- Gentle movement that feels nurturing, not punishing
- Reaching out to one supportive person
- Creating moments of joy, however small

Reflection Questions:
How do your feelings about your body shift with your mood?
What activities bring you joy regardless of how you look?
Who makes you feel accepted exactly as you are?
What would you say to your body if depression weren't clouding your vision?

Remember, **seeking help isn't just okay; it's an act of profound self-care**. Whether through therapy, medication, or a combination of both, professional support can provide crucial tools for managing both depression and body image concerns. Sarah, described therapy as "finally finding someone to help me untangle the knots between my mood and my mirror."

Your journey with depression and body image is deeply personal, and healing doesn't follow a straight line. Some days will feel lighter than others, and that's okay. What matters is that you keep reaching for support from professionals, loved ones, or your own developing self-compassion practice.

Remember, your body and mind deserve gentleness, especially on heavy days. You're not alone in this experience, and there is always hope, even when depression tries to convince you otherwise.

Finding Peace in the Present Moment: Mindfulness Techniques

Last autumn, I sat cross-legged on my meditation cushion, feeling particularly frustrated with my body. As the morning light filtered through my window, I remembered something a wise teacher once told me: "The body isn't something to be fixed – it's something to be listened to." That morning became a turning point in my understanding of how mindfulness could transform our relationship with our bodies.

Mindfulness offers us a different way of being with our bodies – one that doesn't demand change or perfection but instead invites curiosity and compassion. Rachel, shared how years of scrutinizing her reflection had exhausted her. Through mindfulness, she learned to experience her body not as an image in the mirror but as the home that carries her through life. "For the first time," she told me, "I could feel my body instead of just seeing it." Imagine the power in this.

Let me share some practices that have helped many women begin this journey:

The Body Whispers Practice:

Find a quiet moment and comfortable position. Starting with your toes, move your attention slowly through your body. Notice sensations without trying to change them the warmth in your feet, the pressure where your body meets the chair, the rhythm of your breath. This isn't about fixing or judging; it's about listening with curiosity and care.

Mindful Meals:

Before your next meal, take three deep breaths. Notice the colors on your plate, the aroma of your food, and the way your body feels before eating. As you eat, slow down enough to taste each bite fully. Notice when you feel satisfied without judgment. This practice helps us rebuild trust in our body's natural wisdom about food and nourishment.

I remember Sofia's story, how she transformed her morning routine from a battle with the mirror into a mindful check-in with herself. "Instead of immediately criticizing what I see," she shared, "I now take a moment to thank my body for carrying me through another day. Sometimes I still struggle, but mindfulness gives me a way back to peace."

DAILY MINDFULNESS MOMENTS:

- Morning Body Gratitude: Before rising, name three things your body helped you do yesterday.
- Mindful Movement: Feel the sensation of your feet touching the ground as you walk.
- Breath Awareness: Take three conscious breaths whenever you catch your reflection.
- Evening Body Scan: End your day with a gentle journey through your body, offering kindness to each part.

. . .

Reflection Questions:

*What sensations do you notice in your body
right now?*
*How does your relationship with your body shift when
you focus on feeling rather than looking?*
*What would change if you approached your body with
curiosity instead of judgment?*
*Where in your body do you feel most connected? Most
disconnected?*

REMEMBER, mindfulness isn't about forcing positive feelings or denying difficult emotions. It's about creating space to experience whatever arises with gentleness. Some days, you might feel deep appreciation for your body; others, you might struggle. Both experiences are valid; mindfulness helps us hold them with compassion.

Maria's journey with mindful walking particularly touches me. She described how feeling the strength in her legs and the rhythm of her breath helped her appreciate her body's capabilities rather than its appearance. "Each step became a reminder that my body is my ally," she shared, "not my enemy."

This practice of present-moment awareness offers us a refuge from the constant evaluation and criticism our bodies often face. It reminds us that our appearance doesn't determine our worth and that true body acceptance begins with being present with ourselves, exactly as we are right now.

Rewiring Our Body Stories

The other evening, while engaging in a workshop, I watched as a participant had what she called her "lightbulb moment." She realized that her thought, "I look horrible today," wasn't a fact, it was a story she'd been telling herself for so long that it felt like truth. This is where the power of Cognitive Behavioral Therapy (CBT) lives: in those moments when we begin to see that our thoughts about our bodies are not unchangeable facts, but stories we can learn to rewrite.

Understanding CBT: A Dance of Thoughts, Feelings, and Actions

Imagine your mind as a three-part harmony, where thoughts, feelings, and behaviors create life's melody. Cognitive Behavioral Therapy (CBT) shows us how these three elements dance together, each one influencing the others.

Think about slipping on that outfit you love. If the thought "I look terrible" crosses your mind, you might change clothes (behavior), leading to feelings of sadness or frustration. But here's the beautiful part - by changing any part of this dance, you can shift the whole pattern. Maybe you challenge that critical thought, keep wearing the outfit (behavior), and discover new feelings of confidence blooming.

It's like having access to three different doorways into the same room, you can enter through your thoughts, your actions, or your feelings, and each entrance affects the entire space.

Think of your mind as a path through a forest. The negative thoughts about your body are like well-worn trails, the ones you've walked so many times that they seem like the only way through. CBT helps us notice these paths and, more importantly, shows us how to create new ones. I remember working with Maya, who would automatically think "Everyone is staring at how big I am" whenever she entered a room. Through CBT, she learned to pause and ask, "Is this thought helping or hurting me? What evidence do I actually have?"

Let me share some gentle ways to begin this journey of thought transformation:

. . .

When you catch a negative body thought, imagine you're a kind but curious detective. Ask:

- Where did this thought come from?
- What evidence supports or challenges it?
- What would I say to a friend having this thought?
- What's a more balanced way to see this situation?

The Experiment Garden:

Start small, like planting seeds. Picture yourself as a gardener of your own growth. Just as no one expects a seed to become a flower overnight, we can nurture change through gentle, mindful steps.

Imagine turning on your favorite song in the privacy of your living room. Maybe your mind whispers, "I look ridiculous" or "I can't dance." That's okay, those thoughts can be there. Like clouds passing overhead, you can notice them and still keep moving. Feel the rhythm in your feet, the way your shoulders naturally want to sway. No mirrors, no judgment; just you and the music.

Or perhaps it's that sleeveless top hanging in your closet, the one that makes your inner critic pipe up. Instead of listening to those familiar fears "Everyone will stare" or "My arms aren't good enough", try wearing it at home first. Water your confidence with small moments of bravery. Notice how the fabric feels against your skin, how the breeze feels on your shoulders.

Each Small Step Counts

- Dance for just one song in your kitchen
- Wear that sleeveless top while watering your plants
- Notice the difference between what your fears predict and what actually happens

- Celebrate these tiny victories, they're growing something beautiful

Remember, like any garden, growth happens gradually. Some days you might take two steps forward, other days one step back. That's all part of the natural process.

Sarah's breakthrough moment happened after years of avoiding swimming. She believed everyone would judge her body, therefore she would not swim. Her first "experiment" was simply sitting by the pool in her swimsuit with a trusted friend. "Nothing terrible happened," she shared, laughing. "In fact, the only person who had been judging me all those years was myself."

Daily CBT Practices:

- Morning Thought Check: Notice your first body-related thought of the day
- Evidence Gathering: List three facts that challenge your negative body beliefs
- Alternative Story Writing: Practice creating more balanced body thoughts
- Success Spotting: Note moments when you challenged old body beliefs

Reflection Questions:

What's your most persistent negative thought about your body?

Where did you learn this thought?

What would your life be like if you didn't believe this thought?

What's a gentler way to think about your body?

Remember, changing thought patterns isn't about forcing positivity it's about finding more balanced, truthful ways to see ourselves. Some days this work will feel easier than others, and that's perfectly normal. What matters is our willingness to question these old stories and open ourselves to new possibilities.

The tools of CBT (thought records, behavioral experiments, and evidence evaluation) are like different keys on a ring. Not every key will fit every lock, but having multiple tools gives us options for unlocking new ways of seeing ourselves. Start with what feels manageable, knowing that each small step builds toward lasting change.

Your body story isn't set in stone. With patience, practice, and self-compassion, you can begin to write new chapters that reflect not just how your body looks, but all that it does, feels, and helps you experience in this world.

Learning to Dance with Discomfort

Yesterday, during a particularly challenging moment with my own body image, I remembered something profound a mentor once told me: "The goal isn't to never have difficult feelings about your body, it's to learn how to live fully even when those feelings visit." Sometimes, thoughts and actions related to our bodies are so ingrained that it can feel nearly impossible to change them. If that's your reality right now, that's okay - there's still a lot you can do to feel better. My mentor's wisdom captures the heart of Acceptance and Commitment Therapy (ACT), an approach that's transformed how many of us navigate our relationship with our bodies.

Imagine having a toolbox for life that helps you navigate both sunny days and storms with equal grace. That's what Acceptance and Commitment Therapy (ACT) offers. At its heart, ACT is like learning to dance with life rather than fight against it. Think of it as mindfulness meets action you learn to accept your thoughts and feelings as they come (even the uncomfortable ones), while staying focused on what truly matters to you. Instead of trying to push away difficult emotions (which often makes them stronger), ACT teaches us that it's okay to feel what we feel while still moving toward our goals and values.

Here's the beautiful truth ACT embraces: being human means experiencing the full spectrum of emotions. When we stop trying to avoid the hard parts of life, we often find more freedom to live fully.

Let me share about Elena, who spent years trying to battle away every negative thought about her body. "It was like playing whack-a-mole with my feelings," she said. "The more I fought them, the more exhausted I became." Through ACT, she learned something revolutionary that she could acknowledge her body anxiety without letting it direct her life's choreography.

The dance of acceptance isn't about giving up or giving in. Instead, it's about creating space for all our experiences while moving toward what matters most. Like Laura who shared how she stopped waiting to "feel confident enough" to go swimming with her children. "My value of being present with my kids became bigger than my fear of being seen in a swimsuit," she explained. "The anxiety didn't disappear, but it no longer got to make the decisions."

LET me share some gentle ways to practice this approach:

The six core processes of ACT offer us different doorways into this work:

1. We practice acceptance by making room for all our feelings
2. We use defusion to see thoughts as thoughts, not absolute truths
3. We stay present instead of getting lost in body worry
4. We remember we're more than our body thoughts
5. We clarify what truly matters to us
6. We take action aligned with these deeper values

The Four A's Practice:

- **Acknowledge:** Notice your body-related thoughts without trying to change them
- **Allow:** Give yourself permission to feel whatever arises
- **Accommodate:** Make room for these feelings while still living your values
- **Appreciate:** Find moments of gratitude for your body's journey

Values Compass Exercise:
Take a moment to consider:

- What matters most to you beyond appearance?
- How might your life be different if you let these values guide you?
- What small step could you take today aligned with these values?

Remember: Values are at the center of this work; they're why we learn these skills in the first place. They give meaning to our struggles and direction to our choices.

DAILY ACT PRACTICES:

- Morning Values Check-in: Connect with what truly matters today
- Thought Noticing: Practice observing body thoughts without getting caught in them
- Present Moment Anchoring: Use your senses to connect with the now
- Committed Action: Choose one value-aligned action despite body anxiety

Reflection Questions:

*What activities have you been postponing until your
    body "looks right"?*

*How might accepting uncomfortable body feelings
    create more freedom in your life?*

*What would you do differently if your values, not your
    body image, led the way?*

*Where can you create more space between a body
    thought and your response to it?*

I remember watching Sarah's transformation through ACT. She described it like learning to swim with the current instead of against it. "My negative thoughts about my body still show up," she shared, "but now they're like weather patterns passing through; I notice them, but I don't let them determine where I go or what I do."

Remember, this journey isn't about reaching a destination of perfect body acceptance. It's about learning to move forward with our values while making space for whatever thoughts and feelings arise. Some days this will feel easier than others, and that's perfectly normal. What matters is our willingness to keep showing up for our lives, even when body image challenges arise.

Your body story is part of your journey, but it doesn't have to be the whole story. Through ACT, we learn to hold our body experiences gently while moving toward what matters most in our lives.

Chapter 5

Coming Home to Our Body's Wisdom: Integrating Intuitive Eating

One crisp autumn day, I found myself at a local farmer's market, surrounded by the vibrant colors of fresh produce. As I wandered through the stalls, sampling ripe apples and fragrant herbs, I felt a deep connection to the food and the people who grew it. It was a stark contrast to the countless times I had mindlessly followed restrictive diets, detached from the joy of eating. This moment was a reminder of the power of intuitive eating – the practice that allows us to reconnect with our body's natural hunger cues and find pleasure in food without guilt or stress.

I think about all the women I've worked with who've shared their complicated relationships with food – the years spent counting calories, following rigid rules, and feeling shame around eating. Like Maria, who remembered the exact moment she realized she couldn't recall the last time she'd eaten something simply because it brought her joy. Or Sarah, who spent decades viewing food as either "good" or "bad" before discovering there was another way.

The journey back to intuitive eating often feels like returning home to a place we never should have left. Our bodies are born knowing how to eat – babies cry when hungry and turn away when full. Somewhere along the way, many of us learned to distrust these internal signals, replacing them with external rules and restrictions that pulled us further from our natural wisdom.

In this chapter, we'll explore how to rebuild trust with our bodies and rediscover the pleasure of eating intuitively. We'll look at practical tools for recognizing hunger and fullness cues, understanding emotional eating, and making peace with food. Most importantly, we'll discuss how to navigate this journey with patience and self-compassion.

Reflection Moment:
*When was the last time you ate something purely
    because it brought you joy?*
*What would it feel like to trust your body's hunger and
    fullness signals?*
*How might your life change if food choices came from
    wisdom rather than rules?*
*What small step could you take today toward more
    intuitive eating?*

Remember, this journey isn't about perfection, it's about reconnecting with your body's innate wisdom and finding freedom in your relationship with food. Let's walk this path together, one mindful bite at a time.

Coming Back to Our Body's Natural Wisdom

Last night, as I prepared dinner, I found myself remembering a conversation with a client who'd spent thirty years following diets. "I know more about calories than I do about what my body actually wants," she said, her voice heavy with exhaustion. That moment captured something I've witnessed countless times – how diet culture can disconnect us from our innate ability to know what, when, and how much to eat.

Think about a baby's relationship with food; they cry when hungry, turn away when full, and never worry about counting calories or carbs. This natural wisdom lives in all of us, though it might be buried under years of food rules and restrictions. Intuitive eating isn't about learning something new; it's about remembering something we were born knowing.

I remember my own lightbulb moment with intuitive eating. After years of following various diets, I found myself at a café, actually tasting my food for the first time in years. Not analyzing it, not calculating its worth in points or calories, just experiencing it. That moment of freedom showed me what was possible when we trust our bodies again.

The Core Wisdom of Intuitive Eating:

- **Rejecting the Diet Mentality:** Like clearing out old clothes that no longer fit, we release diet books, meal plans, and rigid rules that have kept us trapped.
- **Honoring Our Hunger and fullness:** Learning to listen for and respond to our body's gentle (and sometimes not-so-gentle) requests for nourishment.

- **Making Peace with Food:** Removing the moral labels from food – no more "good" or "bad" foods, just different experiences and choices.
- **Discovering Satisfaction**: Allowing ourselves to enjoy food again, finding pleasure in the experience of eating.

This practice makes me think of Maya, who shared how liberating it felt to eat breakfast when she was actually hungry rather than at her predetermined "acceptable" time. Or James, who realized he'd never really tasted his favorite foods because he was always eating them quickly, secretly, wrapped in shame.

DAILY INTUITIVE EATING PRACTICES:

- Morning Body Check-in: Notice your hunger level without judgment
- Meal Presence: Take three deep breaths before eating
- Satisfaction Scale: Notice what foods truly satisfy you
- Permission Practice: Choose one "forbidden" food to eat mindfully

Reflection Questions:

What would it feel like to truly trust your body's hunger signals?

How has diet culture influenced your relationship with food?

What foods bring you genuine pleasure and satisfaction?

What's one food rule you're ready to question?

Remember, this journey isn't about perfect eating – it's about learning to trust yourself again. Some days will feel more intuitive than others, and that's perfectly normal. What matters is your willingness to listen to your body's wisdom, even when diet culture screams otherwise.

The ten principles of intuitive eating offer us guideposts, not rigid rules. They remind us to honor our hunger, respect our fullness, cope with our emotions with kindness, and approach nutrition with gentleness. Each principle invites us back into conversation with our bodies, helping us rebuild trust that may have been damaged by years of dieting.

Think of intuitive eating as coming home to yourself. Unlike the temporary fixes of dieting, this approach offers lasting peace with food. It's about nourishment, not punishment; wisdom, not rules; freedom, not restriction.

Like ancient wisdom passed down through generations, these ten principles of intuitive eating offer a pathway back to our body's inherent knowledge. Each principle serves as a gateway to healing our relationship with food and reclaiming the natural connection we were born with.

1. First, we must release the chains of diet culture, letting go of its false promises like autumn leaves falling from a tree. This rejection of the diet mentality isn't just about stopping diets; it's about reclaiming our power from a system that never served our souls.

2. Our bodies speak to us through hunger, a sacred messenger we've often learned to silence. Honoring this hunger becomes an act of trust, like answering the call of a dear friend who knows exactly what we need. When we listen to these whispers of need, we begin to rebuild trust with our own wisdom.

3. Making peace with food requires the courage to dismantle the walls we've built around certain foods. Like

negotiating peace after a long war, we lay down our weapons of restriction and guilt, allowing all foods to coexist peacefully within our world.

4. The food police - those harsh voices of judgment living in our minds - must be met with compassion and firmly shown the door. These voices aren't our own; they're echoes of diet culture that have taken up residence in our thoughts.

5. Our fullness speaks in gentle waves, like the ebb and flow of tides. Learning to honor these signals means tuning in to the body's natural rhythm, recognizing when we've had enough without fear or judgment.

6. Discovering satisfaction in eating is like rekindling an old love affair - with food, with our bodies, with the simple pleasure of nourishment. This satisfaction factor reminds us that eating isn't just about fuel; it's about joy, connection, and celebration.

7. Our emotions deserve their own space to breathe, to be felt and honored without using food as a bandage. Like learning a new language, we begin to understand what our feelings are truly asking for.

8. Respecting our body becomes a daily practice of acceptance and care, like tending to a garden that doesn't need to be transformed - only nurtured as it is. This body of ours, in all its complexity, deserves our reverence.

9. Movement becomes a celebration rather than a punishment. Like children at play, we rediscover the joy of moving our bodies for the simple pleasure it brings,

free from the burden of calorie-counting and weight
goals.

10. Finally, we embrace gentle nutrition as our guide, not our
ruler. Like a wise elder offering advice, we learn to make
food choices that honor both our health and our
happiness, understanding that nourishment comes in
many forms.

Gentle Reminder: Your body knows how to eat. It's known
since the day you were born. Our work now is simply to clear away
the debris of diet culture and return to that innate wisdom, one
mindful bite at a time.

Learning Our Body's Language

One morning, as I reached for a cookie from the break room at work, I
caught myself mid-motion. The familiar pause came: "Am I actually
hungry, or am I avoiding that difficult email in my inbox?" This
moment of awareness this simple pause can be revolutionary in our
relationship with food. It's like learning to speak a language we once
knew fluently but have forgotten over years of dieting and rushed
meals.

Rachel, shared how she'd spent decades ignoring her body's
signals, eating by the clock, like most of us, instead of her hunger. "I
didn't even know what hunger felt like anymore," she admitted
during a session. "I only knew what time lunch 'should' be." Her
journey back to body awareness began with simple check-ins, like
placing a hand on her stomach before eating and asking, "What is my
body telling me right now?"

Let me share some gentle ways to start reconnecting with your
body's signals:

The Body Wisdom Check-in:

Before eating, take three deep breaths and notice:

- Physical sensations (empty stomach, energy level, light-headedness)
- Emotional state (stressed, happy, anxious, bored)
- Time since last meal
- Type of hunger (stomach hunger vs. mouth hunger)

I remember Maria's breakthrough moment with the Hunger-Fullness Scale. She'd always eaten until her plate was clean, regardless of fullness. Learning to pause mid-meal and check in with her body felt foreign at first, but gradually became second nature. "It's like having a conversation with my body," she shared. "And for the first time in years, I'm actually listening."

Daily Practice Suggestions:

- Morning Body Scan: Notice your natural hunger upon waking
- Meal Pauses: Take three intentional pauses during each meal
- Fullness Checks: Rate your fullness on a scale of 1-10 throughout meals
- End-of-Day Reflection: Notice patterns in your hunger and fullness

Reflection Questions:
What does physical hunger feel like in your body?
How do you know when you're comfortably full?
What emotions trigger the desire to eat when you're
   not physically hungry?
What helps you stay present during meals?

Understanding the difference between physical and emotional hunger is like learning to distinguish between different notes in music. Physical hunger builds gradually, can be satisfied with any food, and leaves you feeling energized. Emotional hunger often comes suddenly, craves specific foods, and might leave you feeling disconnected from your body.

Sophie is a person, who discovered that her afternoon snacking wasn't about hunger at all it was her body's way of asking for a break from her demanding job. This awareness helped her respond more appropriately, sometimes with food if she was truly hungry, but often with a short walk or moment of quiet instead.

Creating Your Hunger-Fullness Journal:

Consider noting:

- Time of day
- Physical hunger level (1-10)
- Emotions present
- What you ate
- Fullness level after eating
- Any insights or patterns you notice

Remember, this isn't about getting it "right" but learning to listen to your body's wisdom again. Some days, you'll feel more in tune than others, and that's perfectly normal. What matters is your willingness to keep showing up for this conversation with your body.

Think of regular meals and snacks as appointments with yourself opportunities to practice this body awareness. Just as you wouldn't expect to learn a new language overnight, be patient with yourself as you relearn your body's natural rhythms and signals.

Your body has been speaking to you all along. Now is the time to quiet the external noise of diet culture and tune back into its wisdom, one meal at a time.

When Food Becomes Our Comfort

One evening, after receiving difficult news, I found myself standing in front of the open refrigerator, not really seeing what was inside. In that moment, I recognized an old pattern seeking comfort in food when my heart felt heavy. This scene plays out in countless kitchens, late at night or during stressful days, when food becomes our attempt to fill emotional holes that really need different kinds of nourishment.

The relationship between emotions and eating is complex and deeply personal. Linda, would often share with me how she'd turn to ice cream every time she felt lonely, finding temporary solace in its sweetness. Then there was Maria, who couldn't face a work presentation without stress-eating beforehand, using food as armor against her anxiety.

Understanding our emotional eating patterns is like learning to read a map of our hearts. Each person's map is different, marked with unique triggers and patterns. I remember working with Sarah, who started keeping what she called her "heart hunger journal." Through her careful observations, she noticed that Sundays were particularly challenging – the quiet afternoon hours often led her to the kitchen, not because of physical hunger, but because of an emptiness that food couldn't really fill.

The first step in navigating emotional eating is recognition. Before we can change any pattern, we need to understand it with compassion and clarity. This means pausing to check in with ourselves before reaching for food, asking gentle questions about what we're really hungry for.

The **HALT** Check-in has become a powerful tool for many women I work with. Before eating, they pause to ask:

- Hungry? (Is this physical hunger?)
- Angry? (What's stirring inside?)
- Lonely? (Do I need connection?)
- Tired? (Would rest serve me better?)

Creating an Alternative Comfort Menu can provide options when emotions run high. Think of it as building a toolkit for your heart. For stress, you might try deep breathing or a gentle walk. When loneliness visits, perhaps calling a friend or writing in a journal could provide the connection you're seeking. Boredom might be better served by engaging in a hobby or learning something new.

Rachel's breakthrough moment in therapy was when she realized her evening snacking were really about processing the day's stress. "Food was my way of debriefing," she shared. "Once I found other ways to decompress like walking while calling a friend the urge to eat became less intense." Her story reminds us that change is possible when we approach it with understanding and patience.

Building a supportive environment is crucial in this journey. This might mean creating a physical comfort corner in your home, stocked with non-food items that soothe and support: a soft blanket, calming tea, favorite books, or art supplies. It's about giving ourselves options for comfort that nourish us in different ways.

Professional support can be invaluable in this journey. Whether through therapy, support groups, or working with specialists who understand emotional eating, reaching out shows courage and commitment to your well-being. Many women find that having professional guidance helps them uncover and address the root causes of their emotional eating patterns.

- Morning Emotional Weather Check: Notice what you're feeling
- Comfort Corner: Create a space with non-food comfort items
- Movement Medicine: Use gentle movement to process emotions
- Connection Rituals: Schedule regular check-ins with supportive friends

Reflection Questions:

What emotions most often lead you to food?
What does food represent in those moments?
What other forms of comfort feel nurturing to you?
How might you show yourself compassion during
  emotional eating moments?

Comfort or emotional eating is a coping strategy that may feel good in the moment but can leave us feeling regretful or uncomfortable later on. After eating in response to emotions, it's common to experience guilt or shame, which can lead to more restrictive behaviors in an attempt to "make up for" the overeating. This sets off a cycle of emotional eating followed by restriction, and it can feel like an unending loop.

Remember, the goal isn't to never eat emotionally—that's not realistic or necessary. Instead, we're learning to expand our emotional coping toolkit, so food doesn't have to carry all the weight of our feelings. Emotional eating patterns are not character flaws; they are attempts to meet very real needs. Whether we turn to food for comfort, to fill a void, or to manage stress, these behaviors are often rooted in unmet emotional needs. Breaking this cycle requires self-compassion and patience as we find healthier ways to cope with emotions, and learn to recognize the difference between physical hunger and emotional cravings. By treating ourselves with kindness, we can gradually replace these patterns with more nourishing ways of meeting our emotional needs.

As we learn to identify and meet these needs in various ways, our relationship with food can become more balanced and peaceful. This journey isn't about perfection; it's about progress and understanding. Each small step toward awareness and self-compassion is a victory worth celebrating.

Rediscovering the Dance of Flavor and Joy

One evening, as steam rose from a pot of simmering soup in my kitchen, I caught myself smiling at the simple pleasure of stirring herbs into the broth. The aroma of fresh basil transported me back to summer gardens, and I realized how long it had been since I'd truly allowed myself to experience the pure joy of cooking and eating. After years of viewing food through the lens of rules and restrictions, this moment felt like coming home to a forgotten pleasure.

Maya, shared how she'd forgotten the taste of her grandmother's empanadas during her years of strict dieting. When she finally allowed herself to make them again, tears streamed down her face at the first bite. "It wasn't just the flavors," she told me, "it was like remembering who I was before food became complicated."

The journey back to food joy is deeply personal and often begins with small moments of curiosity. Like Elena, who started her mornings by really tasting her coffee instead of rushing through it, or Sarah, who began exploring the farmer's market each weekend, letting the colors and textures of fresh produce guide her cooking adventures.

Creating a Joyful Eating Environment

I've learned that the space where we eat can profoundly impact our experience. Some of my clients create what they call "pleasure corners" in their homes – small dining areas with beautiful plates, soft lighting, and perhaps a vase of fresh flowers. Even a simple breakfast can feel special when eaten from your favorite bowl, with a cloth napkin and a moment of gratitude.

The Magic of Mindful Exploration

Approaching food with curiosity can transform every meal into an adventure. Try this: Choose one new ingredient each week to explore. Notice its texture, color, and aroma. How does it change when cooked? What memories or feelings does it evoke? This practice helps us rebuild our natural sense of food pleasure and discovery.

Cooking as a Love Language

There's something magical about creating food with our own hands. I remember watching Claire, who'd struggled with restrictive eating for years, gradually rediscover joy through baking bread. "The first time I kneaded dough," she shared, "I felt connected to generations of women before me. It wasn't about calories anymore, it was about creation and care."

DAILY JOY PRACTICES:

- Morning Flavor Meditation: Really taste your first bite of food each day
- Sensory Exploration: Notice three new things about familiar foods
- Kitchen Play: Try one new recipe or ingredient weekly
- Social Connection: Share a meal with someone you love

Reflection Questions:

What foods bring back happy memories?
How could you make your eating environment more pleasurable?
What new cuisine would you like to explore?

Building a Balanced Relationship

When you eat and digest mindfully, you begin to notice how your body responds to different foods. Larger amounts of non-nourishing foods may leave you feeling unwell; bloated, lethargic, or uncomfortable. This is your body's way of communicating that balance and moderation are key to feeling your best. By tuning into these sensations, you can start to make more conscious choices that honor both your health and your pleasure.

Finding joy in food doesn't mean abandoning nutrition—it means weaving pleasure and nourishment together. Like a beautiful dance, we can move between enjoying a fresh, crisp salad and savoring a rich piece of chocolate cake, knowing there's room for both in a joy-filled relationship with food. Mindful eating allows us to appreciate the flavors, textures, and satisfaction that food provides, without guilt or restriction, creating a healthy balance that supports our well-being.

Creating Food Memories

Some of life's most precious moments happen around food. Whether it's cooking Sunday dinner with family, sharing coffee with a friend, or teaching a child to bake cookies, these experiences create lasting memories that enrich our lives far beyond the nutrients on our plates.

The Art of Mindful Eating

Taking time to truly taste and experience our food can transform even the simplest meal into a moment of joy. Try this practice: Before your next meal, take three deep breaths. Notice the colors and textures on your plate, the aromas rising from your food, the way the first bite feels on your tongue. Let yourself be fully present with the experience.

Remember, rediscovering food joy is a journey, not a destination. Some days you'll feel more connected to this pleasure than others, and that's perfectly normal. What matters is your willingness to stay open to the possibility of finding joy in food again, one mindful bite at a time.

Your relationship with food deserves to be as rich and varied as life itself. By approaching eating with curiosity, creativity, and compassion, we can rebuild a connection to food that nourishes both body and soul.

Chapter 6

Finding Peace in a Scrolling World

You are not the number on a scale. You are the stories you tell yourself. You are the wisdom in your bones. You are your own truth."
– Brene Brown

One evening, as the soft glow of my phone illuminated my face, I caught myself in a familiar spiral. An old friend's vacation photos appeared on my screen – pristine beaches, perfectly angled bikini shots, and that carefully curated happiness that seems to define social media. The familiar ache of comparison crept in, that whispered voice asking why my life, my body, my experiences couldn't match these filtered moments.

I sat with that feeling for a moment, recognizing it as one that visits so many of us in these digital spaces. I thought about Sarah, who shared how she'd spend hours each night scrolling through fitness influencers' posts, each swipe leaving her feeling smaller, less worthy. Or Maria, who couldn't enjoy her own beach vacation because she was too busy trying to capture the "perfect" shot for Instagram.

The relationship between social media and our self-image is complex and often painful. What began as platforms for connection have become stages where we perform versions of ourselves, measuring our worth in likes and followers. I remember working with Emma, who described social media as "a house of mirrors where everything looks distorted, but you can't stop looking."

Yet within this digital landscape, we can learn to navigate with more awareness and self-compassion. Like Claire, who transformed her social media experience by consciously curating her feed to include diverse bodies, authentic voices, and content that made her feel seen rather than insufficient.

Sometimes the bravest act is pressing "pause" on our constant connection. This doesn't mean abandoning social media entirely, but rather learning to use it in ways that serve rather than drain us.

GENTLE PRACTICES FOR DIGITAL BALANCE:

- Morning Minutes: Wait 30 minutes after waking before checking social media
- Content Cleanse: Unfollow accounts that trigger comparison or anxiety
- Reality Checks: Remember that posts are curated highlights, not full stories

- Connection Hours: Set aside phone-free time for real-world connections
- Buffer Before Bed: Give yourself at least 30 minutes before bed without screens or social media.

Reflection Questions:
How does social media impact your body image and self-worth?
What content makes you feel better about yourself? Worse?
What real-life experiences bring you joy that never make it to your feed?
How might your life change with more intentional social media use?

Remember, social media is a tool we get to decide how to use it. Some days we'll navigate it better than others, and that's okay. What matters is developing awareness of how these platforms affect us and making choices that protect our peace.

Your worth isn't measured in likes or followers. It's not captured in filtered photos or carefully crafted captions. It exists in the quiet moments, the messy reality, the authentic experiences that often never make it to our feeds.

As we begin this chapter's exploration of social media navigation, let's approach it with curiosity and compassion, understanding that we're all learning to find our way in this digital age.

Breaking Free: A Pause from Social Media's Body Noise

Last month, I noticed my hands would automatically reach for my phone every time I felt even slightly uncomfortable in my body. During moments when I caught my reflection, after a meal, or even while trying on clothes there I was, scrolling through endless posts of "perfect" bodies, making my own body anxiety worse. It wasn't until I found myself comparing my stomach rolls to a fitness influencer's posed photo that I realized something needed to change.

The signs that we need a social media break often whisper before they shout, especially when it comes to body image. Rebecca, shared with me how she couldn't get dressed in the morning without checking fitness accounts for "body inspiration." Or Michelle, whose body dysmorphia intensified every time she saw perfectly curated gym progress photos. These moments aren't failures they're invitations to pause and reconnect with our real bodies, not the filtered versions we see online.

When Body Comparison Becomes Your Scrolling Companion:

Sometimes the need for a social media break shows up in subtle ways:

- That immediate body check after seeing a swimsuit photo
- The automatic "I should start another diet" thought after seeing before/after posts
- The way you feel about your body before vs. after scrolling
- How you can't eat a meal without thinking about how it would look on Instagram
- When scrolling leaves you feeling depleted rather than connected
- If comparison becomes a constant companion
- When you're more focused on documenting moments than living them
- If your first morning thought is checking social media

I remember Jamie's revelation during her first social media break: "I didn't realize how much I was absorbing unrealistic body standards until I stepped away. Suddenly, I could see my body as it was, not as it 'should' be according to social media."

Creating Your Body-Peace Digital Pause

Think of a social media break like creating a quiet space where your body can exist without constant comparison. Start small perhaps a weekend away from platforms that trigger body anxiety. **Set intentions that focus on body acceptance:**

- How might I feel about my body without constant external influence?
- What would it be like to eat without seeing others' food rules?
- How could I move my body for joy rather than for photos?

Finding Your Way Back to Body Trust

Nature has a wonderful way of helping us reconnect with our bodies authentically. Laura discovered this during her month-long break when she started taking evening walks instead of evening scrolls. "I stopped thinking about how my body looked and started appreciating how it felt strong legs carrying me forward, lungs breathing in fresh air, arms swinging freely."

BODY-POSITIVE ALTERNATIVE ACTIVITIES:

- Morning Body Gratitude: Thank your body for three things it does for you
- Joyful Movement: Dance, stretch, or walk without documenting it
- Mirror Work: Look at yourself with kindness, not criticism
- Real Body Talk: Have honest conversations with friends about body image

Body Image Reflection Questions During Your Break:

- How does your body image shift without social media influence?
- What messages does your body send when you're truly listening?
- How do you feel about your body in moments of genuine presence?
- What would body acceptance look like without external validation?

The Power of Processing Your Body Story

Keeping a body image journal during your social media break can reveal patterns we might miss otherwise. Note how your relationship with your body changes when you're not constantly comparing it to filtered images online.

Sarah's journal entry during her break particularly moved me: "Day 7 without Instagram. Today I wore a swimsuit and actually enjoyed the beach instead of worrying about taking the perfect angle photo. I felt the sun on my skin and the water on my body, and for once, that was enough."

Remember, the goal of a social media break isn't to never return; it's to return with stronger boundaries around content that impacts your body image. It's about creating space to remember how it feels to live in your body without constant comparison and judgment. And it's about tuning into your intuition about the kind of content that brings you joy and meaning.

Your journey back to body acceptance might look different from others, and that's perfectly okay. What matters is taking that first brave step away from the scroll, even if just for a day, to rediscover what it feels like to be in your body without social media's constant commentary.

Creating a Feed That Feeds Your Soul

Last week, during a late-night scrolling session, I found myself caught in the familiar trap of comparison. My thumb moved automatically past images of "perfect" bodies, each swipe leaving a small dent in my self-esteem. Then I paused on a post that felt different – a woman sharing her real body, unfiltered and unapologetic, talking about her journey to self-acceptance. It was like taking a deep breath after being underwater too long.

The art of curating our social media isn't just about decluttering it's about creating a digital space that nurtures rather than diminishes our relationship with our bodies. Mia, described her old Instagram feed as "a highlight reel of everything I thought I should be." After mindfully rebuilding her follow list, she said it felt like "finally finding my tribe of real bodies and real stories."

Understanding our digital environment's impact on body image requires honest reflection. Each post we scroll past leaves an impression, whether we realize it or not. These subtle influences shape how we view our own bodies, either reinforcing negative self-talk or supporting our journey toward acceptance. Taking time to notice these effects can reveal patterns we might have missed.

I remember working with Jamie, who started what she called her "body peace list" tracking how different accounts affected her body image throughout the day. "Some accounts were subtle in their toxicity," she shared. "It wasn't just the obvious before-and-after posts; it was the constant 'body checking' poses and diet talk disguised as wellness."

The process of curating begins with gentle awareness. Take notice of how your body feels as you scroll. Does your shoulders tense when certain accounts appear? Do you find yourself holding your breath or automatically sucking in your stomach? These physical responses often signal content that doesn't serve our well-being.

Creating a more nurturing feed involves both removing what harms and adding what heals. Start by unfollowing accounts that promote restrictive eating, showcase heavily edited bodies, or trigger comparison. Replace them with voices that celebrate diversity, share authentic experiences, and approach body image with compassion and nuance.

Sarah's transformation particularly moves me. She spent years following fitness models and diet accounts, each post a reminder of what she "lacked." During her feed renovation, she discovered accounts celebrating bodies like hers. "For the first time," she shared, "I saw bodies with stretch marks being celebrated, not hidden. It helped me see my own marks as stories, not flaws."

Engagement matters as much as observation. When we like, share, and comment on body-positive content, we not only support creators who promote healing messages, but we also train our social media algorithms to show us more content that nurtures rather than diminishes our self-image.

- Morning Intention: Set a body-kind theme for your scrolling
- Engagement Check: Like and share content that makes you feel good in your skin
- Boundary Setting: Use mute features for triggering content
- Community Building: Connect with others on similar journeys

Reflection Questions:
What kind of content makes your body feel at home?
Which accounts inspire genuine self-acceptance?
How can your social media support your body image healing?
What voices do you want to amplify in your digital space?

Remember, curating your feed is an ongoing practice. It's okay to adjust and readjust as you learn what serves your journey. Some days you might need to mute more accounts, other days you might find new voices that resonate. What matters is creating a space that reflects and supports the relationship you want to have with your body.

Your social media should be a garden of growth, not a museum of impossible standards. Let's plant seeds of self-acceptance, water them with authentic content, and watch how different our digital world can feel when it's aligned with real body peace.

Standing Strong Against Digital Body Hate

Last month, I received a message that made my heart sink. A stranger had taken time out of their day to comment on a photo of me enjoying a beach day, suggesting I "shouldn't wear swimsuits at my size." As I sat there, feeling the familiar sting of shame creep in, I remembered all the women in my practice who've faced similar moments of online cruelty. The landscape of online body shaming is vast and often treacherous. Sometimes it arrives as direct hits, explicit comments about our bodies that land like arrows. Other times, it's more subtle; those "helpful" fitness suggestions or "concerned" messages about health that mask judgment behind false care.

The impact of online body shaming runs deep, affecting how we show up in digital spaces and how we feel about ourselves. Maya, received a series of "before and after" weight loss ads after posting a joyful photo of herself dancing at a wedding. "It's like the internet has an opinion about every inch of our bodies," shared Rachel during a support group session. "One day, someone commented that I was 'brave' for posting a beach photo. I spent hours trying to decide if that was a compliment or an insult disguised as kindness." These experiences highlight how crucial it is to develop strategies for protecting our peace in online spaces.

When faced with body shaming, having a plan can help us respond from a place of strength rather than reaction. Think of it as creating armor; not to hide behind, but to protect your well-being. I remember working with Sofia, who developed what she called her "shame-free screenshot folder." She documented the hate but didn't let it live rent-free in her mind. "Each screenshot became evidence of their problem, not mine," she explained. This approach of documenting while distancing ourselves emotionally can be powerful in maintaining our mental health.

The aftermath of body shaming can feel isolating, but building a strong support system is essential. Creating a circle of support might include trusted friends who understand and validate your experience, online communities that celebrate body diversity, and professional support when needed. Sometimes, standing against body shaming means finding strength in numbers. Sarah shared how her followers rallied when someone left cruel comments on her fitness journey photos. "They didn't just defend me," she said, "they created a wave of body-positive comments that drowned out the hate."

Immediate action steps are crucial when facing online body harassment. This includes documenting harmful messages, blocking negative accounts, using platform tools to report harassment, and stepping away from devices when needed. These practical steps, combined with emotional support, create a comprehensive approach to handling digital body hate.

Self-care becomes particularly vital after experiencing body shaming. Engaging in gentle movement like dance or walking can help reconnect with your body positively. Comfort practices such as wrapping yourself in soft blankets or taking warm baths can provide physical soothing. Speaking kind words to yourself in the mirror and expressing feelings through creative outlets like journaling or art can help process the emotional impact.

Remember, responding to body shaming isn't just about defending yourself – it's about creating ripples of change. Each time we stand up to body hate, we make the digital world a little safer for everyone who comes after us. You get to decide how to handle body shaming in your digital spaces. Some days you might choose to educate, others to block and move on. Both responses are valid.

DAILY PROTECTION PRACTICES:

- Morning Digital Boundaries: Set limits on social media exposure
- Support Check-ins: Connect with body-positive friends regularly
- Documentation System: Keep record of harassment if needed
- Self-care Rituals: Maintain practices that ground you

What words would you say to a friend facing body shaming?

How can you extend that same kindness to yourself?

What boundaries do you need to set in your digital spaces?

Who makes up your support system when things get tough?

YOUR BODY DESERVES to exist in digital spaces without apology or explanation. Through conscious action, strong support systems, and consistent self-care, we can stand together against body shaming, creating corners of the internet where all bodies are welcomed, celebrated, and free from judgment. Remember, someone else's body shame is about them, not you, and you have every right to protect your peace in whatever way serves you best.

Becoming a Voice for Change: Creating Body-Positive Spaces Online

Last week, I posted something that made my hands shake: an unfiltered photo of myself laughing at the beach, rolls, cellulite, and all. The vulnerability felt overwhelming, but the responses brought tears to my eyes. Women began sharing their own unfiltered moments, each one a small act of revolution against the perfectly curated feeds we've grown accustomed to. This moment reminded me of the profound power we hold to transform social media from a source of comparison into a catalyst for healing.

Creating authentic content that celebrates real bodies isn't just about posting photos – it's about sharing the stories that live in our skin. Elena, started documenting her journey of learning to dance again after years of avoiding it due to body shame. Her weekly videos, showing her body moving with joy rather than judgment, inspired hundreds of others to rediscover movement they'd denied themselves. These ripples of influence remind us that our vulnerability can become someone else's permission to exist more fully in their body.

The community aspect of body positivity online creates a powerful network of support and understanding. When Maria first shared her story of recovering from decades of dieting, she found herself surrounded by others who deeply understood her experience. Together, they created a weekly virtual coffee chat where women could discuss their relationships with their bodies openly and honestly. What began as one person's brave share transformed into a healing space for many.

Supporting and amplifying diverse voices in the body-positive community multiplies our impact. I remember watching a video from a plus-size yoga teacher demonstrating modifications for different body types. The comment section filled with grateful responses from people who'd never seen their body type represented in fitness content before. By sharing and engaging with content that shows the beautiful diversity of human bodies, we help create the representation we wish we'd seen earlier in our journeys.

Education plays a crucial role in fostering body positivity online. When we share articles about the history of beauty standards, the impact of diet culture, or the science behind body diversity, we help others understand that their body struggles exist within a larger context. This knowledge can be incredibly freeing, helping people realize that their perceived "flaws" are actually natural, normal variations of human bodies.

The power of hashtags and online movements shouldn't be underestimated. Tags like #BodyPositivity, #AllBodiesAreGoodBodies, and #EffYourBeautyStandards create searchable archives of encouragement and support. These digital gathering spaces allow people to find others who share their experiences and values, creating communities of support that transcend geographical boundaries.

· · ·

- Share unfiltered moments of joy in your body
- Document your body acceptance journey
- Post about activities you once denied yourself
- Celebrate body-positive victories, big and small

Community Building Actions:

- Engage meaningfully with body-positive content
- Create supportive comment sections
- Share resources and educational materials
- Join or host virtual gatherings for body acceptance discussions

Reflection Questions:

What aspect of your body journey might help others feel less alone?

How could your social media presence challenge beauty standards?

What kind of content do you wish you'd seen earlier in your journey?

How might your vulnerability create space for others' healing?

Remember, every post that celebrates authentic bodies, every comment offering support, and every share of body-positive content helps create the cultural shift we need. Your voice, your story, and your journey matter. By sharing them, you help create a digital world where all bodies can exist without apology or explanation.

The impact of your body-positive presence online may reach further than you'll ever know. Someone out there needs to see exactly what you have to share, your real moments, your honest struggles, your authentic celebrations. In a world of filters and perfection, your truth can be the light that helps others find their way home to body acceptance.

Breaking Free from Diet Culture's Grip

"We delight in the beauty of the butterfly but rarely admit the changes it has gone through to achieve that beauty."
— **Maya Angelou**

It was a sunny afternoon when I was meeting with a dear friend over tea, watching tears slip into her cup as she recounted her latest diet attempt. "I'm so tired," she whispered, "of feeling like my body is a problem to solve." Her words hung in the air between us, heavy with the weight of countless similar conversations I'd had with women over the years. Her story echoed my own journey through the maze of diet culture, where each new eating plan promised happiness but delivered only deeper self-doubt.

Diet culture's influence runs through our lives like invisible threads, weaving themselves into our daily thoughts, our social interactions, and even our deepest beliefs about our worth. Maria, spent twenty years believing that if she could just lose those last ten pounds, her life would finally begin. Or Sarah, who realized she couldn't remember the last time she'd eaten a meal without calculating its calories or compensating for it later.

The cost of living under diet culture's rules extends far beyond our relationship with food. It affects how we show up in the world, how we connect with others, and most importantly, how we treat ourselves. I remember the moment in my own journey when I realized I'd spent more time thinking about my body size than about my dreams, my relationships, or the impact I wanted to have on the world.

In this chapter, we'll explore how to recognize diet culture's influence in our lives and, more importantly, how to begin dismantling its power over us. We'll look at practical ways to rebuild trust with our bodies and rediscover the joy of eating without rules or restriction. This isn't just about changing how we eat; it's about reclaiming our right to live fully in our bodies, exactly as they are.

Reflection Questions:
When did you first become aware of diet culture's influence in your life?
What would your relationship with food look like without diet culture's rules?
How much mental space does thinking about food and weight occupy in your day?
What dreams or aspirations have you put on hold while pursuing weight loss?

Remember, breaking free from diet culture isn't about replacing one set of rules with another. It's about returning to our innate wisdom about food and our bodies, wisdom that existed long before we learned to count calories or fear carbohydrates. Let's begin this journey together, with compassion for how we got here and hope for where we're going.

Unmasking the Beast: Diet Culture's Hold on Our Lives

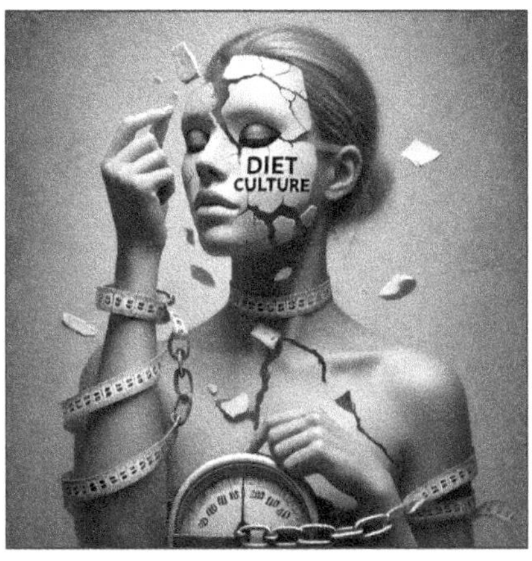

Last week, while cleaning out old journals, I found a diet log from fifteen years ago. Pages filled with calorie counts, "good" and "bad" food lists, and harsh self-criticism brought back memories of years spent believing that controlling my body was the key to happiness. This discovery sparked a conversation with my colleague Emma, who shared how she'd once spent $3,000 on a weight loss program that promised to "fix" her body – a body that was never actually broken.

Diet culture operates like an invisible prison, its bars made of "before and after" photos, weight loss advertisements, and the constant message that our bodies need fixing. This multi-billion-dollar industry thrives on our insecurities, selling everything from appetite suppressant lollipops to extreme exercise programs, all while wrapping their marketing in the deceptive language of "wellness" and "health." Maya, shared how she spent years believing that her worth was inversely proportional to her dress size, each new diet promising the happiness that always seemed just ten pounds away.

The psychological damage of living under diet culture's reign runs deep. In my practice, I've witnessed countless women develop disordered eating patterns while pursuing what they believed was "healthy living." Take Jessica, who began following a "clean eating" program that gradually transformed into orthorexia, her initial interest in nutrition morphing into an obsessive fear of foods deemed "impure." Or Rachel, whose cycle of restriction and binging began with a simple New Year's resolution to "get healthy."

Diet culture's influence seeps into every corner of our lives, from casual lunch conversations about who's eating "good" or "bad" foods to social media feeds filled with before-and-after transformations. It shows up in well-meaning family members who comment on our bodies and in workplace wellness programs that equate health with weight loss. I remember sitting in a coffee shop, listening to three different conversations about dieting happening simultaneously, a stark reminder of how normalized this form of self-restriction has become.

The physical toll of chronic dieting often goes unacknowledged. Our bodies weren't designed for the constant stress of restriction and weight cycling. Linda, developed severe metabolic issues after decades of yo-yo dieting, her body's natural regulatory systems disrupted by years of artificial manipulation. The pursuit of thinness often comes at the cost of our actual health, though diet culture works hard to convince us otherwise.

Signs of Diet Culture's Influence:

- Categorizing foods as "good" or "bad"
- Feeling guilty after eating certain foods
- Believing weight loss will solve life's problems

- Postponing joy until reaching a certain size
- Judging yourself and others based on food choices

Reflection Questions:

What's your earliest memory of feeling your body wasn't "good enough"?

How has diet culture influenced your relationship with food?

What would you do differently if you weren't thinking about your weight?

How much money and time have you spent trying to change your body?

Understanding diet culture's impact is like putting on glasses after years of blurred vision suddenly, we can see clearly how this system has shaped our beliefs, behaviors, and sense of self-worth. This awareness, though sometimes painful, is the first step toward freedom. As one client beautifully expressed, "Once you see diet culture for what it is, you can't unsee it and that's when real healing begins."

Remember, recognizing diet culture's influence in your life isn't about assigning blame, it's about understanding how these external pressures have shaped your relationship with food and your body. This awareness creates space for something new to emerge: a relationship with your body based on respect, trust, and genuine well-being rather than arbitrary standards of acceptability

Dismantling the Diet Myths That Hold Us Captive

Yesterday, while having coffee with a friend, she pulled out a food tracking app and meticulously logged her morning latte, explaining how she needed to "earn" her breakfast through exercise later. This moment crystallized everything wrong with how diet culture has taught us to think about food and our bodies. The simple joy of sharing coffee with a friend had been reduced to numbers in an app, a perfect example of how deeply diet myths have embedded themselves in our daily lives.

The "calories in, calories out" myth might be one of the most damaging oversimplifications in diet culture's arsenal. Elena, has spent years believing this mathematical equation would lead to her "ideal" body. She meticulously counted every calorie, only to find her body responding in ways that defied this simple math. Our bodies are intricate symphonies of hormones, emotions, and biological processes, not vending machines where we insert exercise and extract weight loss.

The good food/bad food dichotomy has created a moral hierarchy around eating that serves no one. I remember working with Sarah, who would have panic attacks in grocery stores, terrified of choosing the "wrong" foods. Years of categorizing foods as either angels or demons had left her unable to trust her own hunger and cravings. "I realized I was spending more time thinking about food's moral value than its ability to nourish and satisfy me," she shared after beginning her healing journey.

The science behind why diets fail tells a compelling story that diet culture doesn't want us to hear - set point theory. Our bodies possess an intricate system of self-regulation, something I explain to clients using the thermostat analogy. Just as your home's thermostat works to maintain a consistent temperature, your body works to maintain its natural weight range. When we try to override this system through restrictive dieting, our bodies fight back with powerful biological responses.

The set point theory revolutionizes how we understand weight regulation. Mary, described her revelation about set point theory as "finally understanding why every diet ended the same way." Like a rubber band that returns to its original shape after being stretched, our bodies have sophisticated mechanisms to protect us from what they perceive as famine, even when that famine comes in the form of a trendy diet plan.

COMMON DIET MYTHS VS. REALITY:

- **Myth:** Weight loss is simple mathematics
- **Reality:** Body weight is influenced by countless factors including stress, sleep, hormones, and genetics
- **Myth:** Some foods are "good," others are "bad"
- **Reality:** All foods can fit into a healthy relationship with eating
- **Myth:** Quick weight loss is sustainable
- **Reality:** Rapid weight changes often trigger biological resistance

Reflection Questions:

How has the "calories in, calories out" myth affected
your relationship with food?
What foods do you consider "forbidden," and how does
that affect your eating?
How has your body responded to past dieting
attempts?
What would eating look like if you trusted your body's
wisdom?

MOVING beyond these myths opens the door to a more peaceful relationship with food and body. Rachel, finally found freedom when she stopped fighting her body's natural weight range. "It's like I finally put down a heavy backpack I didn't even know I was carrying," she shared. Her story reminds us that there's life beyond the confines of diet culture's myths.

Understanding these myths doesn't mean giving up on health – quite the opposite. It means pursuing well-being in a way that works with your body rather than against it. It means choosing movement that brings joy, eating foods that satisfy and nourish, and measuring health by how you feel rather than how you look.

Remember, your body's wisdom runs deeper than any diet plan. When we stop trying to outsmart our biology and start working with it instead, we open ourselves to a more sustainable and peaceful approach to health.

Navigating the Landmines: Spotting and Surviving Diet Culture Triggers

Last Sunday morning, I was enjoying a peaceful breakfast when a weight loss commercial interrupted my favorite show. The familiar before-and-after photos flashed across the screen, accompanied by promises of "a new you." My stomach tightened, a physical reminder of how diet culture can ambush us in even our quietest moments. This experience reminded me of countless similar stories shared in my support groups, where women describe how these unexpected triggers can shake their foundation of self-acceptance.

The landscape of diet culture triggers is vast and often cleverly disguised. Mia, realized her entire social media feed had become a minefield of "wellness" influencers promoting detox teas and workout challenges. "It was like death by a thousand paper cuts," she explained, "each post slowly eroding my self-worth until I couldn't remember what it felt like to be comfortable in my skin."

Family gatherings often become particularly challenging trigger zones. I remember working with Lauren, who dreaded holiday dinners not because of the food, but because of the inevitable commentary about bodies and eating habits. "It's like everyone becomes a nutritionist and personal trainer rolled into one," she shared. The well-meaning but harmful comments about who's lost or gained weight, who's "being good" or "being bad" with their food choices, create an atmosphere thick with judgment and anxiety.

Workplace environments can be equally challenging. Sophie described how her office's "wellness challenge" became a breeding ground for diet culture, with colleagues openly discussing their weights and comparing restricted eating habits. What was meant to promote health had transformed into a competitive arena of body shame and disordered eating behaviors.

Learning to recognize these triggers is like developing a new language – suddenly, you start hearing diet culture's whispers everywhere. But recognition is just the first step; building resilience requires practical strategies and consistent practice.

CREATING A BUFFER ZONE:

- Curate social media feeds to promote body acceptance
- Prepare responses for common triggering situations
- Establish clear boundaries about body and food talk
- Build a support network of like-minded individuals

Rachel, transformed her morning routine after realizing how much diet culture content she consumed before even leaving her bed. She replaced social media scrolling with gentle movement and journaling, creating a protective bubble around her early hours. "It's like putting on armor," she explained, "but instead of protecting me from external threats, it strengthens my internal resolve."

- Social Media: Unfollow, mute, or block content that promotes diet culture
- Family Comments: Prepare kind but firm responses about body autonomy
- Workplace Diet Talk: Redirect conversations or establish professional boundaries
- Advertisement Exposure: Practice media literacy and critical thinking

Reflection Questions:

Where do you encounter diet culture most frequently in your daily life?

What physical sensations arise when you face diet culture triggers?

Which strategies have helped you resist diet culture's influence?

How can you create more body-safe spaces in your life?

Remember, building resistance to diet culture triggers isn't about becoming immune to them it's about developing tools to process and respond to them effectively. As one client beautifully expressed, "It's like learning to walk in the rain. You can't stop the rain, but you can carry an umbrella."

Your journey toward trigger resilience is unique to you. Some days you'll feel stronger than others, and that's perfectly normal. What matters is continuing to build your toolkit of responses and surrounding yourself with support that reinforces your worth beyond your body's appearance.

Creating a life less vulnerable to diet culture triggers takes time and practice, but each small act of resistance builds upon the last. Whether it's unfollowing a triggering account, setting a boundary with family, or simply pausing to question a diet culture message, you're actively participating in your own liberation from these harmful influences.

Coming Home to Food: Building a Peaceful Relationship with Eating

Last night, as I sat down to dinner, I noticed something remarkable in its simplicity: I was actually hungry, and I was looking forward to eating without a shred of guilt or mental calculation. This moment, ordinary as it might seem, represented years of healing my relationship with food. I thought about how far I'd come from the days when every meal felt like a battle between desire and restriction.

The journey toward food peace often begins with a radical idea: what if food wasn't the enemy? Elena, spent twenty years viewing every meal as a potential threat to her weight loss goals. During one of our sessions, she had a breakthrough while eating an orange. "For the first time," she shared, "I wasn't thinking about the calories or sugar content. I was just enjoying how sweet it was, how the juice felt on my tongue. I felt like a child again, before food became complicated."

Building trust with food after years of dieting feels like learning to speak a language we once knew fluently but have forgotten. Our bodies are born knowing how to eat. Somewhere along the way, we learned to distrust these natural signals in favor of external rules and restrictions. I remember working with Sarah, who realized she couldn't remember the last time she'd eaten without consulting a clock or calorie-tracking app.

The practice of mindful eating offers a path back to this innate wisdom. Maya's story particularly touches me, she began her healing journey by simply sitting with her breakfast for five minutes each morning, no phone, no TV, just her and her food. "At first, it felt uncomfortable, almost awkward," she admitted. "But gradually, I started noticing things: how different foods made me feel, what true hunger felt like, when I was actually satisfied."

Emotional eating often emerges as a central challenge in this work. Jamie, used food to cope with the stress of her high-pressure job. Through gentle exploration, she discovered that what she really needed wasn't another snack but moments of genuine rest and connection. "Food was my only tool for self-soothing," she realized. "Learning other ways to care for myself felt like finding new colors to paint with."

DAILY PRACTICES FOR FOOD PEACE:

- Begin meals with three deep breaths
- Notice hunger levels before, during, and after eating
- Eat without screens when possible
- Give yourself permission to enjoy your food
- Practice gentle awareness without judgment

Reflection Questions:

*What would eating feel like without rules or
    restrictions?*
How do different foods affect your energy and mood?
*What emotions trigger the urge to eat when not
    hungry?*
*What forms of nourishment, beyond food, does your
    body crave?*

Remember, healing your relationship with food isn't about achieving perfect eating habits. It's about creating space for both nourishment and pleasure, understanding that both are valid reasons to eat. Some days you'll feel more connected to your body's signals than others, and that's perfectly normal.

The path to food peace often requires support. Working with

professionals who understand both the psychological and physiological aspects of eating can provide crucial guidance. As one client beautifully expressed, "Having someone witness my journey back to trusting food and my body gave me permission to trust myself again."

Your body holds deep wisdom about what, when, and how much to eat. This wisdom hasn't been lost, just buried under years of diet culture's rules and restrictions. With patience, practice, and self-compassion, you can rediscover this natural relationship with food, one meal at a time.

Remember, every meal is an opportunity to practice presence, not perfection. Each time you choose to listen to your body rather than external rules, you strengthen the connection to your innate wisdom about food and nourishment.

Chapter 8

The Revolution of Self-Love

"My body is my home, and I treat it with the love and respect it deserves, one step, one stretch, one breath at a time."
—Jessamyn Stanley

One evening, after a particularly challenging day, I sat in my living room, surrounded by the quiet hum of the night. The weight of self-criticism hung heavily on my shoulders. My mind replayed every perceived flaw and mistake from the day. In that moment, I realized how often I neglected to show myself the same kindness and compassion I freely offered to others. This realization sparked my journey towards self-love, a journey that I want to share with you.

The path to self-love often begins in these quiet moments of recognition, when we finally hear how unkindly we speak to ourselves. Claire, came to this awareness while trying on clothes in a department store fitting room. "I heard myself say things to my reflection that I would never dream of saying to another human being," she shared through tears. **"It was like suddenly hearing a bully's voice, except the bully was me."**

These moments of awakening can feel overwhelming, even painful. Yet they also hold profound potential for transformation. I remember working with Maria, who described her journey to self-love as "learning to become my own best friend instead of my worst critic." She began by simply noticing the harsh internal dialogue that had become her constant companion, then gradually learning to respond with the same gentleness she would offer a dear friend.

Self-love isn't just about positive affirmations or bubble baths, though these can be part of the journey. It's about fundamentally shifting how we show up for ourselves in both easy and difficult moments. It's about building a relationship with ourselves based on understanding, respect, and genuine care rather than criticism and conditional acceptance.

Reflection Questions:

When did you first notice the gap between how you treat others and how you treat yourself?

What would change if you spoke to yourself as kindly as you speak to those you love?

How might your life be different if self-love became your default setting?

What small step toward self-love feels possible today?

As we begin this chapter's exploration of self-love and

empowerment, remember that this journey isn't about reaching a destination of perfect self-acceptance. It's about creating a new way of relating to ourselves, one gentle moment at a time. Let's walk this path together, discovering what it means to truly become our own allies in this journey of healing and growth.

Building the Foundation: The Architecture of Self-Love

One morning, while teaching a workshop on self-love, I watched as a participant raised her hand and asked, "But isn't loving yourself just being selfish?" Her question echoed a common misconception that I've encountered countless times. The truth is, as research shows, self-love represents something fundamentally different from narcissism or selfishness. It's about creating a balanced, healthy relationship with ourselves that allows us to show up more fully for others.

I envision self-love as creating a home within ourselves; one with strong foundations, protective boundaries, and plenty of windows letting in light. This home needs regular maintenance and care, just like any physical structure. The work of building this internal home isn't always easy, but it's profoundly worthwhile. Research has demonstrated that cultivating self-love can significantly reduce anxiety and depression while promoting better physical health outcomes (NCBI, 2013).

The barriers to self-love often feel like locked doors we must learn to open. I remember working with Elena, who struggled to practice self-love in a world that constantly told her she wasn't enough. "It feels like swimming upstream," she shared, "trying to love myself when everything around me suggests I need to change." Her experience reflects the challenge many face in navigating between authentic self-love and the pressure of societal expectations.

The practice of self-love requires both gentle persistence and practical tools. As noted by mental health experts, daily affirmations can serve as powerful instruments for reshaping our internal dialogue

(MentalHealthCenterKids, 2023). Sarah, begins each morning by placing her hand on her heart and speaking three simple words: "I am enough." What started as an awkward ritual gradually transformed into a profound practice of self-acceptance.

Creating boundaries becomes another crucial element in this foundation. Maria's story particularly moves me – she described learning to set boundaries as "finally building walls around my garden of self-worth." She started small, unfollowing social media accounts that made her feel inadequate, and gradually expanded to setting limits in her personal relationships. Each boundary became a brick in her foundation of self-love.

Daily Practices for Building Self-Love:

- Morning affirmations rooted in self-worth
- Gratitude journaling focused on body appreciation
- Boundary setting and enforcement
- Mindful self-compassion exercises

Reflection Questions:

*What does the home of your self-love need most
    right now?*
*Which boundaries would help protect your growing
    self-worth?*
*How do you show yourself love during challenging
    moments?*
*What messages about self-love did you learn
    growing up?*

The journey of building self-love often reveals itself in unexpected moments. Like Rachel, who realized she was practicing self-love when she automatically reached for water after feeling thirsty, a simple act of responding to her body's needs without questioning or judgment. These small moments of self-care accumulate, creating a stronger foundation for deeper self-love.

Remember, as research supports, self-love isn't about achieving perfection or constant positivity. It's about creating a sustainable, nurturing relationship with ourselves that can weather life's challenges. This foundation becomes where we can grow, heal, and truly thrive.

Your journey toward self-love is uniquely yours, but you're not alone in this building process. Each small act of self-kindness, each boundary set, and each moment of self-compassion adds another stone to your foundation. As you continue this work, remember that the goal isn't to build a perfect structure but to create a home within yourself where you can truly belong.

Planting Seeds of Confidence: Growing from Within

Last week, during a group session, a woman named Claire shared something that stopped everyone in their tracks. "I always thought confidence was something other people were born with," she said, "like blue eyes or curly hair. I never realized it was something I could grow." Her words captured a truth I've witnessed repeatedly that genuine confidence isn't about what we're given, but what we cultivate.

The garden of confidence requires rich soil: self-awareness mixed with self-acceptance, watered by supportive relationships. Jennifer, spent years trying to build confidence through external achievements only to find it crumbling at the slightest setback. Her journey toward true confidence began when she started keeping what she called her "truth journal" daily reflections on who she was beneath all the doing and achieving.

"It was like getting to know myself for the first time," she shared. "I started writing about my fears, my dreams, even the parts of myself I'd always tried to hide. Surprisingly, the more honest I became with myself, the more confident I felt." Her experience demonstrates how self-awareness creates the foundation for lasting confidence.

The practice of building confidence often begins with small seeds of self-trust. I remember working with Elena, who started her journey by simply promising herself she would take a five-minute walk each day. "It wasn't about the walk," she explained later. "It was about keeping a promise to myself. Each time I did it, I proved to myself that I could trust my word."

Creating spaces for authentic self-expression becomes crucial in this process. Sarah discovered this through art therapy, finding that each brush stroke helped her express parts of herself for which she'd never had words. "The more I allowed myself to create without judgment," she shared, "the more confident I became in other areas of my life."

Daily Confidence-Building Practices:

- Morning self-appreciation ritual
- Small promise-keeping exercises
- Creative expression without judgment
- Strength acknowledgment journaling

The journey often involves pushing gentle edges of comfort zones. Maya began by speaking up in small group settings before gradually working her way up to giving presentations at work. "Each time I survived something that scared me," she noted, "my confidence grew a little stronger."

Reflection Prompts for Your Confidence Journal:

What makes you feel most alive and authentic?
When do you feel strongest in your own skin?
What small wins have you celebrated lately?
How has your confidence grown over the past year?

Remember, building confidence is like tending a garden; it requires patience, consistent care, and understanding that growth happens in seasons. Some days you'll feel your confidence blooming brilliantly; others, you might need to focus on simply maintaining the roots.

Interactive Exercise: Your Confidence Inventory

Take a moment to reflect and write about:

1. Three qualities you admire in yourself
2. A challenge you've overcome and what it taught you
3. A small goal you can set for this week
4. Someone who makes you feel confident and why

BUILDING confidence from within isn't about becoming someone new – it's about uncovering and trusting who you already are. Rachel discovered when she finally stopped trying to mimic others' confidence and started developing her own quiet, steady self-assurance. "It's like finding your voice," she shared. "Once you hear it clearly, you never want to speak in anyone else's again."

Your confidence journey is uniquely yours. Some days, it might involve speaking up in meetings; other days, it might involve simply choosing to wear what makes you feel good regardless of current trends. What matters is that each small act of self-trust builds upon the last, creating a foundation of confidence that comes from truly knowing and accepting yourself.

Remember, true confidence isn't about never feeling fear or doubt, it's about knowing that you can handle whatever comes your way, even if your hands shake a little while doing it. It's about building a relationship with yourself based on trust, understanding, and gentle persistence.

The Sacred Art of Self-Care: Nourishing Your Soul

Last night, as I lit a candle and settled into my evening ritual of gentle stretching and journaling, I thought about how different this felt from my old understanding of self-care. Years ago, I viewed self-care as indulgent, a luxury reserved for special occasions. Now, I recognize it as something far more profound: a daily practice of honoring my worth and nurturing my spirit.

Maya, came to one of my workshops exhausted from constantly putting everyone else's needs before hers. "I felt guilty even thinking about taking time for myself," she shared. "Like somehow being a good person meant running myself into the ground." Her story reflects a common struggle, the belief that self-care is selfish rather than essential.

The transformation in how we view self-care often begins with a simple realization: caring for ourselves isn't just about bubble baths and face masks (though these can be lovely). It's about building a sustainable relationship with ourselves that honors all aspects of our being. I remember working with Elena, who discovered that proper self-care meant learning to say "no" to commitments that drained her energy. "Each boundary I set," she reflected, "felt like a love letter to myself."

Creating a personalized self-care routine requires us to listen deeply to our own needs. Sarah's journey particularly moves me. She began by simply asking herself each morning, **"What would feel like care today?"** Sometimes the answer was as simple as drinking enough water; other times, it meant taking a mental health day from work. The key was learning to trust and honor her own needs.

Physical self-care forms the foundation of our well-being, but it looks different for everyone. For James, it meant replacing his punishing workout routine with gentle movement that actually felt good. "I realized exercise could be about celebrating what my body can do rather than punishing it for what it isn't," he shared.

. . .

Daily Self-Care Practices:

- Morning check-in with your needs
- Mindful movement that feels joyful
- Quiet moments of reflection
- Nourishing food choices without judgment
- Connection with nature or loved ones

Mental and emotional self-care requires equal attention. Rachel discovered the power of "emotional scheduling," deliberately planning time for activities that feed her soul. "I started treating my emotional needs with the same importance as my work meetings," she explained. "It changed everything."

Reflection Questions:

What activities make you feel truly nourished?
How do you know when you need more self-care?
What stands in the way of prioritizing your needs?
What would your ideal day of self-care look like?

Creating sacred spaces for self-care transforms it from an occasional indulgence into a daily practice. This might mean setting up a corner of your home dedicated to quiet reflection or establishing morning rituals that center you before the day begins. Linda created her "renewal room," a small space where she practices meditation, journaling, and gentle movement.

The ripple effects of consistent self-care extend far beyond our well-being. When we care for ourselves deeply, we model self-respect and boundaries for others. We demonstrate that taking care of ourselves isn't selfish; showing up fully in our lives and relationships is necessary.

Remember, self-care isn't about perfection or following someone else's routine. It's about discovering what truly nourishes you and making space for those practices in your life. Some days, self-care might look like an hour-long meditation; other days, it might be simply remembering to breathe deeply between meetings.

Your self-care journey is uniquely yours. Let it evolve with your needs, knowing that every small act of self-care is an investment in your well-being and an affirmation of your worth. One client beautifully expressed, "When I started treating myself as someone worthy of care, the world started treating me that way too."

The Power of Small Victories: Honoring Every Step Forward

Yesterday morning, I watched as a client's eyes filled with tears when she shared what seemed, at first glance, like a simple achievement, she'd looked in the mirror and, for the first time in years, smiled at her reflection instead of criticizing it. "It feels silly to cry over something so small," she said. But we both knew this moment represented a mountain of internal work, a thousand tiny choices that led to this breakthrough.

These moments remind me how profoundly important it is to celebrate our small wins. Melanie, started keeping her "victory journal," a small notebook where she documented everything from drinking enough water to speaking up in meetings. "At first, I thought I was being ridiculous, celebrating such tiny things," she shared. "But after a month, I could flip through those pages and see how all those small wins had built something remarkable."

Celebrating small wins often requires us to shift our perspective on what constitutes success. Sarah's story particularly touches me. She had always dismissed her daily acts of courage until we started breaking down what it actually meant that she could now eat lunch in the office cafeteria, something anxiety had prevented her from doing for years. Each meal represented dozens of small victories: choosing to stay present, managing anxious thoughts, and trusting her hunger cues.

Creating systems to track and celebrate progress can be simple. Elena developed what she calls her "win jar," a beautiful glass container where she drops small notes documenting her daily achievements. "On hard days," she told me, "I empty that jar onto my bed and read through every win. It's impossible to feel stuck when you can see how far you've come."

Celebrating these victories needs to be as personal as the achievements themselves. I remember working with Lisa, who would send herself congratulatory emails after each therapy session, creating a digital trail of her progress. Another client, James, started taking selfies every time he used positive self-talk instead of criticism, building a visual diary of his growing self-compassion.

DAILY VICTORY PRACTICES:

- Morning intention setting for small, achievable goals
- Evening reflection on three wins, no matter how small
- Gratitude for your body's daily achievements
- Celebration rituals that feel meaningful to you

Reflection Questions:
*What small win have you dismissed recently that
    deserves celebration?*
How has your definition of success evolved over time?
*What would change if you celebrated every step
    forward?*
Who could join you in celebrating your victories?

The practice of documenting growth creates a powerful narrative of transformation. Rachel started a "progress photo album" not of her body, but of moments when she felt proud: the first time she ate dessert without guilt, her first yoga class, the day she donated all her "goal weight" clothes. Each photo told a story of growing self-acceptance.

Remember, celebration isn't just about the big moments, it's about honoring every step that moves you closer to self-acceptance and empowerment. Some days, the win might be simply choosing to be gentle with yourself when old patterns of self-criticism arise. On other days, it might be taking a bold step toward a long-held dream.

Interactive Victory Tracking:
Create your personal celebration system:
1. Choose a method that resonates (journal, jar, photos, etc.)
2. Set aside daily time for recording wins
3. Plan meaningful ways to celebrate milestones
4. Share victories with supportive people in your life

Your growth journey deserves to be witnessed and celebrated, especially by you. Each small win is a thread in the tapestry of your transformation, creating a story of resilience, courage, and self-discovery. As one client beautifully expressed, "When I started celebrating my small wins, I realized there's no such thing as a small victory in the journey of becoming yourself."

Chapter 9

Living Your Body Peace Every Day

"I am not free while any woman is unfree, even when her shackles are very different from my own."
— **Audre Lorde**

One chilly winter morning, I stood in front of my closet, overwhelmed by the sheer number of clothes yet unable to find something that made me feel confident and comfortable. The pressure to dress a certain way, to conform to societal standards, weighed heavily on me. I realized that the key to feeling good in what I wore wasn't about keeping up with trends or fitting into a particular size but understanding my body and choosing clothes that empowered me. This chapter is dedicated to helping you find that same sense of confidence and comfort in your daily attire.

The journey to dressing our bodies with kindness often begins with letting go not just of clothes that don't fit, but of the stories we've been told about how we "should" look. Linda, kept a collection of "someday" clothes, sizes smaller than what she currently wore, hanging like promises or perhaps threats in her closet. The day she donated those clothes became a turning point in her relationship with her body. "It felt like giving myself permission to exist now, not in some imagined future," she shared.

Our daily choices about what to wear can either be acts of warfare or acts of peace with our bodies. I remember working with Elena, who started her "comfort revolution," systematically replacing any piece of clothing that made her feel restricted or self-conscious with options that allowed her to move, breathe, and live freely. "I realized I'd been wearing clothes like armor," she reflected, "when I needed to wear them like a friend."

The practical reality of dressing our bodies with love requires more than just good intentions it demands a shift in how we approach our wardrobes and our morning routines. This chapter will explore concrete strategies for creating a closet that serves you, developing an authentic personal style, and navigating the challenges of shopping and dressing in a world that often seems designed for only certain body types.

Reflection Questions:

What messages do your clothes send to your body?

*How would you dress if comfort and joy were your
only criteria?*

*What pieces in your wardrobe make you feel most like
yourself?*

*What would change if you dressed for the body you
have today?*

As we explore practical daily living, remember that how we dress our bodies is deeply personal and politically powerful. Whenever we choose comfort over constraint, authenticity over conformity, we make a statement about our right to exist exactly as we are.

Dressing Your Truth: Finding Freedom in Your Wardrobe

Last Saturday, I watched as Maria stood in front of her mirror, wearing a bright yellow dress she'd always loved but never dared to wear in public. "I've been saving it," she admitted, "for when I felt worthy enough." That moment crystallized something I've witnessed countless times, how deeply our clothing choices connect to our sense of worth and belonging.

The conversation about body shapes and "flattering" clothes often misses the point. While understanding your body's unique architecture can be helpful, it shouldn't become another set of rules that restrict your joy. Sarah, spent years following every guideline for "dressing a pear shape" until she realized she felt most alive in the very styles she'd been told to avoid. **"The most flattering thing I can wear," she now says, "is whatever makes me feel like myself."**

Comfort has become my non-negotiable criterion for clothing, but this wasn't always the case. I remember the years spent squeezing into too-tight jeans and suffering through days in uncomfortable shoes because I thought that's what looking "put together" required. Now I understand that true style emerges from a place of physical ease. As one client beautifully expressed, "When my clothes feel like a friend rather than a fight, my confidence naturally follows."

The landscape of body-positive fashion is finally expanding, though we still have far to go. It reminds me of Elena's joy when she discovered brands like Summersalt and Girlfriend Collective, seeing bodies like hers celebrated in their campaigns. "It wasn't just about the clothes," she shared. "It was about finally feeling seen." These companies aren't just selling garments; they're challenging the narrative about who deserves to feel beautiful.

Creating a personal style that truly reflects you requires unlearning as much as learning. Rachel's journey particularly moves me – she started by removing every piece of clothing that made her feel less than wonderful. "It was scary at first," she admitted. "My closet looked empty. But then I realized I finally had space to discover what I actually loved, not just what I thought I should wear."

PRACTICAL WARDROBE WISDOM:

- Start with comfort as your foundation
- Choose fabrics that feel good against your skin
- Build from your favorite pieces
- Let go of clothes that don't serve you now

Style Exploration Questions:

- What outfit makes you feel most like yourself?
- Which clothes give you energy versus drain it?
- What would you wear if no one was judging?
- How does your current wardrobe reflect or hide your true self?

The process of building a confidence-supporting wardrobe often begins with permission – permission to exist in your current body, permission to take up space, permission to express yourself fully. Maria, started her journey by simply trying on everything in her closet and asking one question: "Does this feel like home?"

INTERACTIVE WARDROBE REVIEW:

1. Touch each piece in your closet
2. Notice your immediate body response
3. Sort into three piles:
"Yes!" (Makes you feel amazing)
"Maybe" (Needs consideration)
"No" (Ready for release)

Remember, your style is as unique as your fingerprint. While understanding general principles about cut, color, and proportion can be helpful, they should never override your personal comfort and joy. As one client wisely noted, "The most important thing my clothes need to fit is my spirit."

Your body deserves to feel at home in its clothing, to move freely, to breathe easily, to express itself authentically. This might mean breaking some traditional "fashion rules." It might mean wearing colors you've been told aren't "flattering" or styles that don't "suit your shape." But if these choices bring you joy and comfort, they are exactly right for you.

Creating a wardrobe that supports your confidence isn't about following trends or rules, it's about building a collection of clothes that help you feel like the most authentic version of yourself. Some days this might mean soft, flowing fabrics that feel like a gentle hug; other days, it might mean bold prints that express your inner vibrancy. What matters is that your choices come from a place of self-respect and celebration rather than restriction and shame.

Creating Your Sanctuary: Building a Home That Holds You

One Sunday afternoon, while sorting through a stack of old magazines in my living room, I had what I now call my "enough moment." Flipping through pages filled with diet tips and before-and-after photos, I suddenly realized how these seemingly innocent materials had whispered inadequate messages into my daily life. This wasn't just about decluttering it was about creating a space that genuinely honored and supported my journey toward body peace.

The process of transforming our homes into body-positive sanctuaries often begins with subtraction. Rachel, described the day she removed her bathroom scale as "breaking up with a toxic relationship." She noticed how that simple act changed her morning routine from judgment to gentle self-greeting. "Without the scale telling me my worth for the day," she shared, "I could finally hear my voice."

Creating spaces that nurture rather than diminish us requires intentional choices. Maya's transformation of her bedroom particularly moves me. She replaced her full-length mirror (which she'd primarily used for body checking) with a smaller one at face height, surrounded by positive affirmations written in bright colors. "Now, when I look in the mirror," she explained, "I see my smile first, not my perceived flaws."

The power of visual messaging in our homes cannot be underestimated. I remember working with Elena, who created her "celebration wall," a collection of photos, artwork, and quotes that reminded her of her body's strength and resilience. "I included pictures of myself laughing with friends, hiking mountains, holding my children," she shared. "It helps me remember that my body is much more than how it looks."

CREATING YOUR BODY-POSITIVE SPACE:

- Remove diet-culture materials
- Add affirming artwork and messages
- Create comfortable, welcoming spaces
- Incorporate elements of nature and peace

Designing self-care corners is another powerful way to honor our bodies. Sarah transformed a tiny corner of her apartment into what she calls her "peace station," a comfortable chair, soft blanket, and basket filled with books about body acceptance and self-love. "Having this dedicated space," she noted, "reminds me that taking care of myself isn't optional; it's essential."

HOME ENVIRONMENT ASSESSMENT QUESTIONS:

- What messages do your surroundings send about bodies?
- Where in your home do you feel most at peace?
- What items trigger negative body thoughts?
- How could your space better support your healing?

The process of creating a body-positive home environment extends beyond decoration to functionality. Consider how your space supports your body's needs and comfort. One client redesigned her kitchen to make cooking more enjoyable and accessible, replacing diet cookbooks with ones that celebrated nourishment and pleasure in eating.

INTERACTIVE SPACE TRANSFORMATION:

1. **Body-Peace Room Audit:**
   - Note items that support/hinder body acceptance
   - Identify spaces that need more comfort/joy
   - List potential additions that would promote healing

2. **Creating Comfort Zones:**
   - Designate areas for rest and reflection
   - Add elements that engage positive senses
   - Include items that remind you of your worth

REMEMBER, transforming your space is a gradual process. Start with one room or even one corner. As Linda discovered, "Changing my environment helped change my internal landscape. Each positive change in my space reflected a step toward accepting myself."

Your home should be a refuge from the world's constant messages about how bodies "should" look. It should be where you can breathe deeply, move freely, and exist without judgment. Sometimes, this means making bold changes like Jill, who replaced her collection of fitness magazines with art supplies and began filling her walls with her creative expressions of body acceptance.

Consider how each room in your home could better support your journey. Your bathroom needs more messages of self-love, or your bedroom could use softer lighting and more comfortable seating. Your kitchen may feel more welcoming with plants and positive affirmations about nourishment rather than calorie counts.

Creating a body-positive home environment isn't about achieving perfection – it's about building a space that supports your healing and growth. Let your home become a physical manifestation of the gentle, accepting relationship you're building with your body.

Standing Your Ground: Protecting Your Peace from Body Critics

One sunny afternoon, I found myself at a family gathering, where an aunt's seemingly innocent question about my weight landed like a stone in still water, creating ripples of discomfort that lasted long after the party ended. Her voice, dripping with what she called concern, reminded me why setting boundaries isn't just helpful – it's essential for survival in a world that often treats our bodies as public property.

The journey of boundary-setting often begins with a moment of clarity. Sofia, shared with me about the day she finally responded to her mother's constant commentary about her size. "I had rehearsed what to say a hundred times," she shared, "but when the moment came, I simply said, 'Mom, I love you, but my body isn't up for discussion.' The look of surprise on her face told me she'd never considered that she needed permission to discuss my appearance."

CREATING scripts for these challenging moments can be incredibly empowering. I remember working with Elena, who kept a small notebook of prepared responses for different situations. For family gatherings: "I appreciate your concern, but I'm not discussing my body today." For workplace comments: "I prefer to keep conversations professional." For social situations: "I'm focusing on how I feel, not how I look."

The art of using "I" statements transforms these interactions from confrontational to constructive. Consider how different these approaches feel:

Instead of: "You're always commenting on my weight!"

Try: "I feel hurt when my body becomes a topic of discussion."

One client, Amara, found power in her "pause and redirect" technique. When faced with body criticism, she would take a deep breath, acknowledge the comment without engaging with its content, and smoothly change the subject. "It's like being a river," she explained. "Instead of fighting the current, I flow around the obstacles."

BOUNDARY-SETTING STRATEGIES:

- Prepare clear, calm responses
- Practice deep breathing for difficult moments
- Identify your non-negotiable limits
- Plan exit strategies when needed

The support of allies becomes crucial in maintaining these boundaries. Rosa, created what she called her "body peace pact" with close friends. They agreed never to discuss weight loss, diets, or body criticism, instead focusing on celebrating what their bodies could do and feel.

Reflection Questions:

Who makes you feel safe in your body?
What comments trigger the strongest emotional response?

Practice Scenarios for Building Confidence:
1. **Family Gathering Response**:
"I know you care about me, but comments about my body aren't helpful."
2. **Workplace Boundary**:
"I'm focusing on my professional contributions, not my appearance."
3. **Friend Group Standard**:
"In our friendship, I'd like to celebrate our bodies rather than critique them."

REMEMBER, setting boundaries isn't about being unkind; it's about protecting your peace and fostering relationships based on respect rather than appearance. As one client beautifully expressed, "Every boundary I set is a love letter to myself."

Creating a support network becomes essential in maintaining these boundaries. Consider joining body-positive communities where your boundaries are understood and respected. These spaces can provide the validation and encouragement needed when facing criticism.

Your body is your home; you have every right to protect it from unwanted commentary. Some days, you'll feel stronger in maintaining these boundaries than others, and that's perfectly normal. What matters is your commitment to creating a life where your body is respected, not scrutinized.

As we navigate these conversations, remember that changing long-established patterns takes time. Sometimes, setting a boundary means deciding not to share space with someone any longer, especially if continuing that relationship no longer serves your well-being. Be patient with yourself as you learn to speak up, and celebrate each time you successfully maintain a boundary, no matter how small it might seem. It's important to honor your needs and recognize that boundaries are not just about limiting others; they're about creating space for your own growth, peace, and self-respect.

Navigating the Professional World in Your Body

One Monday morning, as I prepared for a significant presentation, I caught myself doing that familiar dance in front of the mirror: adjusting, critiquing, and wondering if I looked "professional enough." This moment reminded me of how many women start their workdays negotiating not just with their calendars but also with their reflections. The corporate world often feels like a stage where our bodies are part of the performance, creating an exhausting double consciousness of being both performer and critic.

The unspoken rules about professional appearance weave into every aspect of our working lives. Alexandra, an amazing top notch executive shared how she spent years trying to make herself smaller in her power suits before realizing that her presence, not her size, commanded respect. "I used to think success meant fitting into a certain image," she reflected. "Now I know it means fitting into my authenticity." Her journey mirrors what many women face: the constant pressure to conform to conventional beauty standards while trying to be taken seriously for their expertise.

Creating a professional wardrobe that serves as armor rather than constraint becomes crucial in navigating these waters. I remember working with Sofia, who transformed her relationship with work clothes by asking one simple question: "Does this garment support my success today?" This simple shift in perspective helped her build a wardrobe that prioritized comfort and confidence over conventional expectations. She discovered that well-fitted basics in comfortable fabrics could look just as professional while allowing her to focus on her work rather than her appearance.

The intersection of professionalism and body image often creates complex dynamics, particularly in male-dominated fields. Maria, is a tech executive who faces constant commentary about her appearance in meetings. She developed what she called her "professional boundary toolkit," ready responses for redirecting appearance-focused conversations back to her expertise. Her strategy included specific phrases and body language that helped her maintain her dignity while asserting her professional values.

Professional presence extends beyond clothing to how we carry ourselves in workplace settings. The practice of confident body language standing tall, maintaining eye contact, and using intentional gestures – can significantly impact how we feel in professional spaces. These physical practices aren't about changing our bodies but about inhabiting them more fully and confidently.

Reflection Questions:
How does your work environment impact your body image?
What would professional confidence feel like in your body?
Where do you need stronger boundaries around appearance?
What messages about "professional bodies" do you need to challenge?

The stories of women reclaiming their professional power continue to inspire profound change. Elena's journey particularly moved me; she stopped wearing uncomfortable heels after twenty years because she realized her ideas, not her height, elevated her presence in meetings. This simple yet powerful decision reflected a deeper truth: our professional value isn't measured by our adherence to beauty standards.

Creating a sustainable professional presence requires developing practices that honor both our career goals and our body's needs. This might mean keeping comfortable shoes at your desk, scheduling regular movement breaks, or establishing clear boundaries around appearance-focused conversations. These aren't just comfort measures; they're strategic decisions that support our ability to do our best work.

Remember, your professional journey shouldn't require compromising your relationship with your body. By building strategies that honor your career goals and your body's needs, you can navigate professional spaces with greater confidence and authenticity. As one client beautifully expressed, "The most professional thing I can do is show up as my whole, authentic self – body and all."

Chapter 10

Honoring Life's Transitions

"Beauty begins the moment you decide to be yourself."
— **Coco Chanel**

It was a crisp autumn morning when I sat down with my friend Emily, who was glowing with the excitement of her first pregnancy. As she sipped her herbal tea, she confided in me about the emotional rollercoaster she was experiencing. "I never realized how much my body would change," she said, her voice tinged with both awe and trepidation. Emily's feelings mirrored many women navigating the beautiful yet challenging pregnancy journey. This chapter addresses the unique body image considerations during pregnancy, offering support and practical advice to help you embrace this transformative time.

The journey through life's significant transitions often changes our relationship with our bodies. Sofia, shared pregnancy as "learning to trust my body in an entirely new way." Maria, spoke about her post-mastectomy journey and how it taught her that healing isn't just physical; it's deeply emotional, too. These moments of transformation demand a special kind of gentleness in ourselves.

Our bodies tell stories of our lives, the challenges we've faced, and the strength we've discovered along the way. I remember working with Rosa, who struggled with the changes menopause brought to her body until she began viewing this transition as a powerful new chapter rather than an ending. "Each hot flash," she joked, "is my inner fire growing stronger."

These special considerations whether pregnancy, illness, injury, aging, or recovery, ask us to expand our definition of body acceptance. They invite us to find new ways of understanding and caring for ourselves during times when our bodies might feel foreign or challenging.

Reflection Questions:
How have life's transitions affected your relationship
    with your body?
What wisdom has your body shared during times of
    change?
Where do you need extra gentleness right now?
How might this current challenge be teaching you
    about self-acceptance?

As we explore these considerations, remember that each woman's journey is unique. There's no "right" way to navigate these transitions, only your way. Let's walk this path together, holding space for the challenges and the profound growth these experiences can bring.

The Sacred Journey: Body Image During Pregnancy

One morning, as I sat with a pregnant client who was tearfully examining her new stretch marks in my office mirror, I was reminded of how pregnancy asks us to rewrite our entire relationship with our bodies. "I know these marks mean my baby is growing," she whispered, "but why is it so hard to accept these changes?" Her vulnerability echoed the complex emotions many women experienced during this transformative time.

The science of pregnancy reveals an incredible orchestra of changes. Hormones like estrogen and progesterone surge through our bodies, not just supporting our growing babies but profoundly affecting our emotional landscape. Sophia, described her pregnancy hormones as "riding waves in an unfamiliar ocean." Some days brought tears of joy; others brought unexpected anxiety about her changing body.

These physical transformations serve vital purposes, though society only sometimes helps us see them that way. I remember working with Maria, who struggled with her pregnancy weight gain until we reframed each pound as evidence of her body's wisdom in nurturing her baby. "Each time I step on the scale," she eventually shared, "I try to thank my body for knowing exactly what my baby needs."

The pregnancy journey often illuminates the gap between medical necessity and societal expectations. While healthcare providers emphasize the importance of healthy weight gain, typically 25-35 pounds for women with a normal BMI, social media continues to celebrate "belly-only" pregnancies and post-birth "bounce backs." As one client noted, "It feels like I'm supposed to be pregnant but only in the most aesthetically pleasing way."

Creating rituals of connection with your changing body can become a powerful antidote to these pressures. Consider these gentle practices:

THE PHYSICAL CHANGES of pregnancy include:

- Stretch marks (affecting up to 90% of pregnant women)
- Fluid retention and swelling
- Breast changes
- Skin changes and the "pregnancy glow"
- Posture adjustments as your center of gravity shifts

Daily Body Connection Rituals:

- Morning or evening belly massage with nourishing oils
- Gentle stretching that honors your new center of gravity
- Mindful moments to feel your baby's movements
- Photography that celebrates your changing shape

Ana, transformed her morning routine into celebrating these changes. "Instead of critiquing my reflection," she shared, "I started greeting my changing body with gratitude. 'Thank you, stretch marks, for making space for my growing baby. Thank you, swollen ankles, for supporting us both.'"

Reflection Questions:

*How has pregnancy changed your relationship with
   your body?*

*What messages about pregnant bodies do you need to
   challenge?*

*Where do you need more support in accepting these
   changes?*

*What wisdom is your pregnant body sharing
   with you?*

Practical Support Strategies:

1. **Creating Comfort:**

- Invest in comfortable, supportive clothing
- Set up relaxation spaces in your home
- Gather props (pillows, yoga blocks, meditation cushions) for rest and movement

2. **Building Support:**

- Connect with other pregnant women
- Share feelings with understanding friends

REMEMBER, pregnancy isn't just about physical changes, it's a profound emotional and spiritual journey. One client beautifully expressed, "Pregnancy taught me that my body isn't just something to look at; it's something to marvel at."

Your pregnant body is doing exactly what it needs to do, precisely how it needs to do it. Some days, you'll feel radiant and powerful; others, you might feel uncomfortable and uncertain. Both experiences are valid parts of this journey.

Consider starting a pregnancy journal where you can document not just the physical changes but the emotional ones, too.

Many women find that looking back on these reflections helps them appreciate the incredible journey their bodies have undertaken.

Remember, every pregnancy is unique, just as everybody is unique. Your journey doesn't need to look like anyone else's to be perfect for you and your baby.

The Fourth Trimester: Honoring Your Postpartum Journey

Last week, I sat with a new mother who was struggling to recognize herself in the mirror six weeks after giving birth. "No one told me it would be like this," she whispered, gesturing to her softer belly and the dark circles under her eyes. Her words echoed a truth many women face: the postpartum period often feels like navigating uncharted waters without a map.

The physical landscape of the postpartum body tells a story of incredible transformation. Our bodies, which spent nine months expanding to create life, don't simply snap back like elastic. Rosa, found an unexpected peace when her midwife explained that the uterus takes at least six weeks just to return to its pre-pregnancy size.

"Understanding the science behind my body's changes," she shared, "helped me be more patient with my healing."

The reality of postpartum changes includes:

- Hormonal fluctuations affecting mood and body composition
- Decreased skin elasticity and stretch marks
- Changes in breast size and shape, especially with breastfeeding
- Softening of the abdominal area as muscles heal
- Pelvic floor adjustments

I remember working with Elena, who transformed her bathroom mirror into a gratitude board, covering it with sticky notes celebrating her body's achievements: "These stretch marks held my baby. These breasts nourish new life. This soft belly cushions my child's head when we cuddle."

Creating a nurturing postpartum care routine becomes essential. Consider these gentle practices:

Daily Postpartum Care Rituals:

- Warm baths with healing herbs
- Gentle belly massage with nourishing oils
- Pelvic floor exercises when cleared by your healthcare provider
- Restorative rest whenever possible

The pressure to "bounce back" can feel overwhelming. Sofia, found freedom in removing all her pre-pregnancy clothes from sight. "Instead of torturing myself with what used to fit," she explained, "I invested in a few pieces that made me feel comfortable now."

Reflection Questions:

*What has your body accomplished in creating and
birthing life?*

*How can you show gratitude to your healing body
today?*

What support do you need in this fourth trimester?

*What messages about postpartum bodies do you need
to release?*

Practical Postpartum Support:

1. **Physical Care:**
   - Invest in supportive garments that comfort rather than constrict
   - Practice gentle movement when ready
   - Prioritize nutrient-rich foods that support healing
2. **Emotional Support:**
   - Connect with other postpartum mothers
   - Share feelings with understanding friends
   - Consider working with a postpartum doula

It is important to recognize that many new mothers, in the midst of caring for their newborns, often neglect their own needs. The focus on caring for the baby can become all-consuming, leaving little room for self-care. But postpartum recovery requires attention to your own well-being as well. It's essential to remember that you cannot pour from an empty cup.

Recommendations for Self-Care and Asking for Help:

- **Ask for help:** Don't be afraid to lean on others—your partner, family members, friends, or postpartum support networks. Accepting help is a sign of strength, not weakness. Whether it's for household chores, a meal delivery, or simply someone to hold the baby while you rest, asking for assistance allows you to recharge.

- **Take breaks:** It's okay to step away from baby duties for a short time. Take a walk outside, enjoy a warm bath, or just sit in silence for a few minutes to reconnect with yourself.
- **Take care of your emotional health:** Emotional well-being is just as important as physical healing. If you're feeling overwhelmed, consider talking to a therapist who specializes in postpartum care, or join a new mom support group where you can share experiences with others who understand.

Stories of women finding peace with their postpartum bodies often involve a shift in perspective. Claire's journey particularly moves me. She began photographing her postpartum body not to document its "flaws" but to celebrate its strength. "Each mark, each change," she shared, "is evidence of the most powerful thing I've ever done."

Remember, your postpartum body is not a problem to be solved; it's a testament to your strength and capacity for creation. Some days you'll feel strong and capable; others, you might feel vulnerable and changed. Both experiences deserve gentle acknowledgment.

CREATING YOUR POSTPARTUM SANCTUARY:

- Set up nursing/feeding stations with water and snacks for you
- Gather comfortable, soft clothing that feels good on your skin
- Create restful spaces where you can bond with your baby
- Keep supportive resources within easy reach

Your postpartum journey is uniquely yours. While social media might show carefully curated "snapbacks," real postpartum recovery happens in quiet moments of self-compassion and gradual healing. As one mother beautifully expressed, "My body might be different now, but so am I – stronger, wiser, and more amazed by what women's bodies can do."

Honoring the Body Through Illness and Pain: A Journey of Resilience

Living with a chronic illness or pain transforms our relationship with our bodies in profound and complex ways. During a support group session one afternoon, Sarah shared something that resonated deeply: "Some days, my body feels like a stranger speaking a language I can't understand." Her words captured the essence of navigating body image while managing chronic conditions: the constant dialogue between acceptance and challenge, between what was and what is.

The physical manifestations of chronic illness/pain create a unique landscape for body image. Conditions like rheumatoid arthritis, lupus, or multiple sclerosis bring not just symptoms but fundamental changes to how we move through the world. These changes affect everything from daily activities to how we see ourselves in the mirror. The unpredictability of symptoms, the visibility of physical changes, and the invisible battle of chronic fatigue all shape our body story in ways that challenge traditional narratives of body acceptance.

Living with fibromyalgia has taught me to navigate pain and rethink my relationship with my body. I used to see my pain and fatigue as a betrayal; now I understand my body isn't fighting against me, it's fighting for me, doing its best under challenging circumstances. This shift in perspective marked a turning point in my journey, transforming my approach to self-care and body acceptance.

Creating a compassionate dialogue with our bodies becomes essential when living with chronic illness and pain. Rosa discovered this truth while managing lupus. She developed what she called her "daily body check-in," a gentle practice of listening to her body's needs without judgment. Some days, this meant celebrating the ability to brush her hair independently; other days, it meant honoring her body's need for complete rest.

The practical aspects of maintaining a positive body image while managing chronic illness and/or pain require creative adaptation. Many women find success in modifying traditional self-care practices to suit their needs. Living with MS, Maria transformed her morning routine into a series of gentle rituals that honored her body's limitations and capabilities. She replaced harsh exercise with gentle stretching, created a simplified skincare routine that didn't exhaust her energy, and learned to pace her daily activities.

Support becomes crucial in this journey. Finding communities of others who understand the unique challenges of maintaining body acceptance while managing chronic illness can provide both validation and practical strategies. These connections remind us that we're not alone in navigating these complex waters. One support group member beautifully said, "In sharing our struggles, we also share our strength."

Reflection Questions:

How has chronic illness changed your relationship with your body?

What wisdom has your body shared through this journey?

Where do you need more gentleness in your self-care routine?

What would acceptance look like today?

Stories of women finding peace with their bodies while managing chronic illness often involve redefining strength. Carla's journey with rheumatoid arthritis led her to discover new ways of moving and being in her body. Through adaptive yoga and gentle movement practices, she found that strength isn't always about power; sometimes, it's about persistence and showing up for yourself day after day.

Remember, living with chronic illness or pain doesn't diminish your worth or beauty. Your body's story includes challenging chapters but also incredible resilience, adaptation, and wisdom. One client said, "My body may not work like it used to, but it works hard for me every day, and that deserves celebration."

Creating a supportive environment becomes essential. This might mean adapting your living space to serve your needs better, surrounding yourself with people who understand you, and developing routines that honor your body's rhythm. It's about building a life that supports your physical and emotional needs.

Your journey with chronic illness/pain and body image is uniquely yours. Some days will feel more challenging than others, and that's okay. What matters is continuing to approach yourself with compassion, celebrating your body's resilience, and honoring its need for care and understanding.

The Art of Aging: Embracing Our Evolving Story

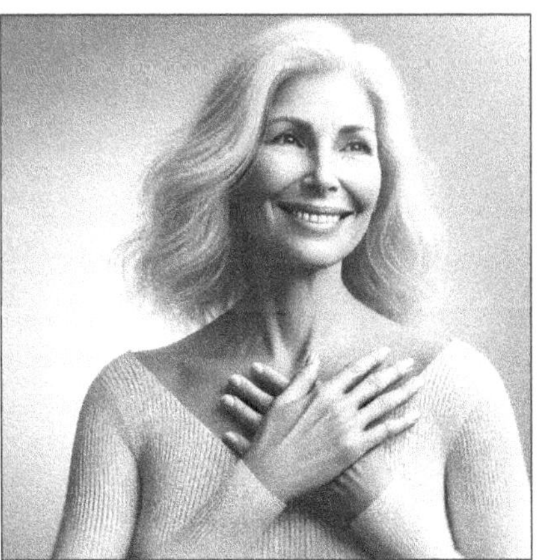

One morning, while teaching a workshop, a silver-haired woman raised her hand and shared something profound: "I spent forty years

fighting my reflection," she said, "until I realized these wrinkles are
my life's poetry written on my skin." Her words captured the essence
of what it means to age gracefully, not in denial of change, but in
celebration of our continuing story.

The science of aging reveals a complex tapestry of natural
transitions. Our bodies, wise and ever-adapting, undergo various
changes:

- Skin loses elasticity due to decreased collagen production
- Gray hair emerges as melanin production decreases
- Metabolism shifts affect body composition
- Muscle mass naturally decreases without resistance
  training
- Bone density gradually changes, especially post-
  menopause

Rebecca, transformed her morning ritual from a battle with her
reflection to a moment of gratitude. "Each line around my eyes," she
shared, "represents thousands of times I've laughed. Why would I
want to erase that history?"

The journey of accepting these changes often requires us to
challenge deeply ingrained societal messages. I remember working
with Elena, who stopped dyeing her gray hair after thirty years.
"The first few months were terrifying," she admitted. "But now I see
my silver streaks as my crown of wisdom. I've earned every single
one."

Creating nurturing practices that honor our aging bodies
becomes essential. Here are a few ways to embrace aging with grace.

Daily Rituals for Aging Grace:

- Gentle morning stretches to maintain flexibility
- Strength training to preserve muscle mass

- Nourishing skincare that celebrates rather than fights aging
- Mindful movement that respects your body's changing needs

The physical aspects of aging deserve tender care and attention:

1. **Strength Preservation:**
- Regular resistance training
- Balance exercises
- Functional movement practice

2. **Nutritional Support:**
- Antioxidant-rich foods
- Adequate protein intake
- Hydration focus

My friend Krista comes to mind; at sixty-five, she started strength training and uncovered a whole new relationship with her body. "I stopped focusing on how my arms looked," she shared, "and celebrated what they could do. Every push-up feels like a victory."

Reflection Questions:

What wisdom has aging brought to your life?
How has your relationship with your body evolved?
What messages about aging do you need to challenge?
What strengths have you discovered in this stage of life?

The stories of women embracing their age inspire profound shifts in perspective. Margaret's journey particularly moved me. She began photographing her changing face every year on her birthday, not to critique but to celebrate. "Each photo tells a story," she explained, " of survival, of joy, of life fully lived."

Creating an Aging-Positive Environment:

- Surround yourself with images of diverse, aging bodies
- Follow social media accounts that celebrate aging naturally
- Create spaces that support your changing needs
- Gather with other women who embrace their age

Remember, aging doesn't happen to us; it's something we get to do. Not everyone receives this gift. As one client beautifully expressed, "Every gray hair, every laugh line, every age spot is evidence that I'm still here, still living, still growing."

Your aging journey is uniquely yours. While society might push anti-aging products and "solutions," true grace comes from accepting and celebrating each stage of life. Some days, you'll feel this acceptance more strongly than others, and that's perfectly normal.

CONSIDER STARTING AN "AGING GRATITUDE" practice:

- Thank your body for its continued strength
- Celebrate new wisdom gained
- Honor the experiences written on your skin
- Appreciate the depth and richness age brings to life

As we age, we don't become less, we become more. More wise, more experienced, more complex in our beauty. Your body isn't betraying you by aging; it's carrying you forward into new chapters of your story.

Chapter 11

Finding Your Tribe: Creating Circles of Support

"We don't have to do it all alone. We were never meant to. True belonging only happens when we present our authentic, imperfect selves to the world." —Brene Brown

One evening, as I scrolled through my social media feed, I stumbled upon a post from a vibrant community of women celebrating body positivity. The post showed women of all shapes, sizes, and backgrounds smiling and supporting each other. It was a stark contrast to the usual posts that promote unrealistic beauty standards. The sense of belonging and acceptance radiated from the images, capturing my attention and drawing me in. This moment highlighted the importance of finding and joining body-positive online and offline communities to foster a supportive network where you can thrive.

The power of community in healing our relationship with our bodies cannot be overstated. Rosa, shared that she found her first body-positive support group after years of feeling isolated in her journey. "Walking into that room," she shared, "was like finally exhaling. These women understood me without explanation." Her experience mirrors what many women discover when they find their tribe, the profound relief of being seen and accepted exactly as they are.

Creating spaces where we can be authentic about our body image struggles transforms individual healing into collective empowerment. I remember working with Elena, who started a small gathering in her living room that grew into a weekly circle of women supporting each other's journeys toward body acceptance. "We laugh, we cry, we celebrate each small victory," she explained. "Most importantly, we remind each other that we're not alone in this."

The journey to finding your community often begins with small, brave steps. Sometimes, it's joining an online group, and other times, it's attending a local workshop or meeting. What matters isn't where you start but that you begin reaching out, creating connections that nurture your growth and healing.

Reflection Questions:

What areas of your life would most benefit from more support right now?

In what settings have you felt most accepted in your body?

What would your ideal supportive community look and feel like?

As we explore ways to build and nurture supportive communities, remember that every strong circle starts with one person reaching out to another. Your search for connection could be the beginning of something transformative, not just for you but for others seeking their own tribe.

Finding Your People: The Search for Body-Positive Spaces

Last week, during a virtual body-positive meetup, a woman shared how she'd spent years feeling like an island, alone in her struggle with body acceptance. "Finding this group," she said, her voice thick with emotion, "was like discovering a continent of people who spoke my language." Her words resonated deeply, reminding me how transformative it can be when we finally find our people.

The digital landscape offers countless opportunities for connection in the body-positive space. Social media platforms have become modern gathering places where communities flourish under hashtags like #BodyPositivity and #AllBodiesAreGoodBodies. Shelley, discovered her first body-positive community through Instagram. "I started by following just one account," she shared, "and it led me to this incredible network of women celebrating their bodies exactly as they are." These online spaces can be stepping stones to deeper connections and in-person communities.

Local communities often provide the tangible support that online spaces can only partially replicate. I remember working with Elena, who started attending a monthly body-positive coffee meetup in her neighborhood. "There's something powerful about sitting across from someone who gets it," she explained. "The virtual hugs are nice, but the real ones hit different." These face-to-face connections create opportunities for authentic sharing and immediate support that can be profoundly healing.

The process of finding the right community requires careful consideration and intuition. Only some spaces that claim to be body-positive truly embody these values. Rosa discovered this when she joined what appeared to be a supportive group but promoted restrictive behaviors under the guise of wellness. "I learned to look beyond the surface," she shared. "Now I pay attention to how a community makes me feel – do I leave feeling uplifted or drained?"

WHEN EVALUATING POTENTIAL COMMUNITIES, consider these essential elements:

- The language used in discussions
- The diversity of bodies represented
- The handling of difficult conversations
- The boundaries and safety measures in place
- The overall atmosphere of support versus competition

Active participation in these communities can transform your journey from solitary to shared. Maria found her voice by commenting on others' posts, sharing her story, and eventually organizing local meetups. "Each step felt scary," she admitted, "but each one also made me feel more connected, more seen."

Reflection Questions:

What kind of support do you most need right now?
How do you want to feel in your chosen community?
What values are non-negotiable for you in a support group?
How might you contribute to creating a more supportive space?

Building meaningful connections within these communities takes time and courage. Start small by introducing yourself in an online group or attending one local event. Remember that everyone in these spaces started as a newcomer, often feeling just as nervous and hopeful as you might feel now.

Consider creating a community assessment checklist:
1. Values alignment
2. Inclusive representation
3. Respectful communication
4. Clear boundaries
5. Genuine support
6. Growth opportunities

Finding your body-positive community might take time, and that's okay. As one client beautifully expressed, "Finding your people is like finding pieces of yourself you didn't know were missing." Trust that the right community will feel like coming home to a place where your body, story, and journey are welcomed and celebrated.

Nurturing Support at Home: The Family Connection

Last Sunday, during a family dinner, my niece announced she was "being good" by skipping dessert. The table fell silent as I gently suggested we avoid labeling food as good or bad. This moment highlighted how deeply diet culture influences our closest relationships and the importance of creating supportive environments where body acceptance can flourish.

The journey of educating loved ones about body positivity often begins with small, meaningful conversations. Rebecca, shared how she transformed her family dynamics by sharing her own story of healing from body shame. "At first, they didn't understand," she shared. "But something shifted when I explained how their comments about weight affected me. They began to see how their words carried weight beyond the dinner table."

Creating new patterns of communication within families requires patience and persistence. Elena found success by introducing what she called "appreciation practice" at family gatherings. Instead of commenting on appearances, family members shared what they appreciated about each other's character, achievements, or kindness. "It was awkward at first," she admitted, "but now our conversations have much more depth and meaning."

Modeling body acceptance within our close relationships becomes a powerful tool for change. I remember working with Sofia, who decided to stop participating in family diet talk. "Every time someone started discussing their latest weight loss attempt, I would redirect the conversation to something more meaningful," she explained. "Eventually, others started following my lead." Her quiet revolution transformed how her family approached body image discussions.

The home environment plays a crucial role in fostering body acceptance. Maria transformed her apartment into a "body peace sanctuary." She removed magazines promoting diet culture, hung artwork celebrating diverse bodies, and created spaces that welcomed comfort rather than judgment. "My home became a place where everyone could breathe easier in their bodies," she shared.

Building supportive family dynamics often requires addressing deeply ingrained patterns.

Consider these approaches:
   - Open discussions about how body comments affect mental health
   - Setting clear boundaries around body talk
   - Celebrating non-appearance-related achievements

- Creating new family traditions that don't center on appearance or food guilt

The process of educating loved ones takes time and compassion. Sarah found success by gradually sharing educational resources, starting with simple articles and working up to more in-depth discussions about body acceptance. "I had to remember that they were learning just like I had been," she reflected.

Reflection Questions:

What body-positive changes would you like to see in your family dynamics?

How can you better communicate your needs for support?

What family traditions might need updating to be more body-inclusive?

Where do you need to set stronger boundaries with loved ones?

Creating a supportive environment extends beyond words to actions. Consider establishing family practices that celebrate all bodies:

- Regular movement activities focused on joy rather than calorie-burning
- Meals that emphasize connection and culture, rather than restriction
- Celebrations that honor achievements beyond physical appearance
- Open discussions about media messages and body diversity

Remember, changing family dynamics is a gradual process. One client wisely noted, "It's like turning a large ship; it happens degree by degree, but eventually, you're heading in a completely new direction."

Your role in fostering body acceptance within your family circle is powerful. Through consistent modeling, gentle education, and clear communication, you can create an environment where everyone feels valued beyond their appearance. As another client beautifully expressed, "When I started treating my body with respect, it gave others permission to do the same."

Leading with Love: Becoming a Body-Positive Light

One afternoon, during a casual lunch with colleagues, I noticed a young intern hesitate before joining our table, clearly uncomfortable in the office environment. Without drawing attention, I shifted my chair to make space, smiled warmly, and continued our conversation about recent projects rather than the usual diet talk. Being a body-positive role model sometimes means creating subtle shifts that make spaces more welcoming for everyone.

The journey of becoming a body-positive influence often begins with our own healing. Linda, transformed her workplace culture not through grand gestures but through consistent, quiet rebellion against diet culture. "I stopped participating in Monday morning diet talk," she shared. "Instead, I would share stories about weekend adventures or new skills I was learning. Gradually, others began following suit, and our conversations became richer, more meaningful."

Modeling authentic self-acceptance ripples out into our communities in powerful ways. Elena discovered this when she started responding to negative self-talk, whether her own or others', with gentle curiosity rather than judgment. "When someone says something harsh about their body," she explained, "I ask them to consider where that thought came from and whether it serves them. It opens up such important conversations about how we've learned to view ourselves."

The practice of being a body-positive role model extends beyond personal interactions into how we show up in the world. Maria, a teacher, realized her influence when a student thanked her for never commenting on anyone's appearance or food choices. "I hadn't even realized the impact of what I wasn't saying," she reflected. "Sometimes being a role model means breaking the cycles of body commentary we've inherited."

Creating safe spaces for others to explore their body acceptance journey becomes essential to this role. Consider these approaches:

- Responding to body-negative comments with compassion
- Sharing your own journey when appropriate
- Celebrating diverse body experiences
- Modeling boundary-setting around body talk

The power of consistent, positive representation cannot be understated. Sarah found that simply posting unfiltered photos of herself enjoying life in her body inspired others to do the same. "It wasn't about being perfect," she shared, "it was about being real and showing others they could be too."

Reflection Questions:
*How can you model body acceptance in your daily
    life?*
*What messages about bodies do you want to share
    with others?*
*Where do you have opportunities to challenge body
    negativity?*
*How can you create more inclusive spaces in your
    sphere of influence?*

Being a body-positive role model involves both personal practice and public stance:

- Use language that celebrates body diversity
- Share stories of body acceptance and healing
- Offer support without focusing on appearance
- Model healthy boundaries around body talk

In Public Spaces:

- Advocate for inclusive policies
- Challenge discriminatory practices
- Create welcoming environments for all bodies
- Share resources and education about body acceptance

Remember, being a role model doesn't mean being perfect. As one client beautifully expressed, "The most powerful thing I can model is how to be gentle with ourselves when we struggle." Your journey, including the challenges and victories, can light the way for others seeking their own path to body acceptance.

Consider starting small but staying consistent:

- Challenge one body-negative comment each day
- Share one body-positive resource each week
- Create one inclusive policy or practice in your sphere
- Offer one piece of non-appearance-based support daily

Your influence as a body-positive role model grows through authentic, compassionate presence. By consistently choosing love over judgment, acceptance over criticism, and inclusion over exclusion, you help create a world where all bodies can thrive.

Creating Circles of Trust: Building Safe Spaces for Body Talk

One evening, during a community gathering, I watched as a woman hesitated before sharing her story. The room fell silent, not with judgment but with deep attention. "I've never said this out loud before," she began, her voice trembling. That moment crystallized the profound importance of creating spaces where vulnerability is met with understanding and acceptance. These safe spaces become sanctuaries where honest conversations about body image can flourish.

The architecture of safe spaces requires careful consideration and intentional design. Sofia, shared how she transistioned her weekly book club into what she called a "body peace circle." She started each meeting by establishing simple but powerful guidelines: speaking from personal experience, listening without trying to fix, and holding each other's stories with care. These basic principles created a foundation where authentic sharing could flourish. Over time, her small group became known as a place where people could bring their whole selves, including their struggles and victories with body image.

Building trust within these spaces happens gradually, like watching a garden grow. Elena, who facilitated body-positive support groups, learned to start each session with what she called "connection moments," brief sharing circles where participants could voice their current feelings without fear of judgment or advice. These small moments of being heard created the safety needed for deeper conversations later. She found that consistent, predictable structures helped participants feel secure enough to explore vulnerable topics.

The practice of maintaining safe spaces requires constant attention to group dynamics and individual needs. Maria discovered this while running online body-positive forums. She developed clear guidelines for communication, ensuring that everyone's voice could be heard while maintaining respect and confidentiality. Her groups became known for their warmth and inclusivity, where members felt safe enough to share their deepest struggles with body image and self-acceptance.

Creating an environment of genuine inclusivity means actively considering diverse experiences and perspectives. Rachel realized her body-positive discussion group wasn't truly accessible to all bodies, so she began by examining the physical space – ensuring comfortable seating options for different body sizes, considering accessibility needs, and creating quiet spaces for those who needed breaks. These practical considerations sent a powerful message about who was welcome in the space.

Reflection Questions:
What makes you feel safe enough to share your truth?
How can you contribute to creating safer spaces?
What boundaries need to be in place for open
   dialogue?
How might you make your spaces more inclusive?

The success of safe spaces often lies in the details of how they're maintained and nurtured over time. Regular check-ins with participants, clear protocols for handling difficult moments, and consistent review of group agreements all contribute to maintaining the integrity of these spaces. As one participant beautifully expressed, "It's not about never making mistakes; it's about how we handle them when they happen."

Remember, creating safe spaces isn't about perfection, it's about consistent intention and care. By fostering environments where authentic dialogue can flourish, you help create the conditions for collective transformation. These spaces become catalysts for healing, understanding, and growth in our journey toward body acceptance.

Creating Change: Leading Body-Positive Movements

Last month, while watching a group of women organize their first body-positive workshop at my office building, I witnessed the power of grassroots initiatives. What started as a small idea during a coffee shop conversation blossomed into a monthly gathering that now draws dozens of participants. Their success reminded me that meaningful change often begins with one person seeing a need and having the courage to address it.

The landscape for body-positive initiatives is vast and varied, offering countless opportunities for impact. Sofia, who transformed her workplace culture by introducing "Wellness Wednesdays" not focused on weight loss or appearance, but on genuine self-care and acceptance. She started small, with lunchtime discussions about media literacy and body image, but the ripple effects spread throughout the company. Soon, the HR department was revising policies to be more size-inclusive, and the break room conversation shifted from diet talk to discussions about personal growth and achievement.

Building successful initiatives requires careful planning and authentic connection to community needs. Elena discovered this while developing a body-positive program for her local high school. "I spent weeks just listening," she shared. "I talked to students, teachers, and parents about their concerns and hopes. The program we created together was so much richer because it addressed real needs, not just my assumptions about what people wanted." Her approach demonstrates the importance of grounding our initiatives in genuine understanding and collaboration.

Partnering with existing organizations can amplify impact and provide crucial support. Maria found success by connecting with local mental health organizations and wellness centers. Together, they created a network of resources and support that reached far beyond what any single group could achieve alone. This collaborative approach expanded their reach and brought diverse perspectives and expertise to their initiatives.

The practical aspects of organizing body-positive events require both vision and attention to detail. Consider these essential elements:

- Clear objectives and measurable goals
- Inclusive venue selection and setup
- Diverse representation in speakers and materials
- Accessible pricing and scheduling
- Follow-up support and resources

Reflection Questions:
What needs do you see in your community?
How could you use your unique skills to create
    change?
What partnerships might strengthen your initiatives?
How will you measure success beyond numbers?

Sustaining momentum in body-positive initiatives requires ongoing evaluation and adaptation. Rachel's monthly workshop series succeeded because she consistently gathered feedback and adjusted the format to better serve participants' needs. "Each session taught us something new about what people needed," she explained. "We learned to be flexible while keeping our core message of body acceptance constant."

Remember, leading body-positive initiatives isn't about creating perfect programs; it's about fostering spaces where healing and growth can occur naturally. As one organizer beautifully expressed, "Sometimes the most powerful moments happen in the conversations between scheduled activities."

Your role in creating change might start small, but its impact can be profound. Whether you're organizing workplace discussions, community workshops, or online support groups, your efforts contribute to a larger movement toward body acceptance and healing. Start where you are, use what you have, and trust that your authentic commitment to this work will guide its growth.

The Power of Voice: Sharing Your Journey to Light the Way

Last week, during a community gathering, a woman stood up and shared her story for the first time. Her voice trembled at first, but as she spoke about her journey to body acceptance, strength filled her words. The room held its breath, recognizing the courage it takes to transform personal struggle into shared wisdom. By the end, three other women had tears in their eyes, finally seeing their own experiences reflected in someone else's truth.

The decision to share our stories often begins with recognizing their potential impact. Rosa, who started by writing private journal entries about her relationship with her body shared "I didn't plan to share them, but one day I realized that keeping my healing to myself meant others might feel as alone as I once did." Her Instagram post about learning to accept her post-pregnancy body resonated with thousands of women who saw their own struggles reflected in her words.

Crafting an authentic narrative requires both courage and careful consideration. Elena spent months reflecting on her journey before sharing it at a women's wellness workshop. She focused not just on the challenges but on the moments of breakthrough that led to healing. "I wanted people to see both the struggle and the hope," she shared. "Because sometimes knowing someone else made it through gives us permission to believe we can too."

Finding your voice and platform takes time and often evolves naturally. Maria began by sharing brief thoughts on her personal Facebook page, then gradually expanded to writing blog posts about her experience with chronic illness and body acceptance. "Each time I shared, someone would reach out privately to say, 'Me too,'" she explained. Those connections showed me that vulnerability creates bridges between hearts."

THE PROCESS of sharing your story involves several key elements:
- Identifying pivotal moments in your journey
- Reflecting on lessons learned
- Considering your audience's needs
- Choosing appropriate platforms for sharing

Reflection Questions:
*What parts of your story might help others feel less
    alone?*
Which moments of transformation could inspire hope?
*How can you share authentically while maintaining
    boundaries?*
What platform feels most natural for your voice?

Creating safe spaces for storytelling becomes crucial in this work. Sarah organized monthly "Story Circles" where women could share their body acceptance journeys in a supportive environment. "We set ground rules about confidentiality and non-judgment," she noted. "These boundaries helped people feel secure enough to be vulnerable."

Remember, sharing your story isn't about crafting a perfect narrative; it's about offering your authentic truth as a light for others. As one woman beautifully expressed after sharing her journey, "I realized my story wasn't just mine anymore. It became a thread in a larger tapestry of healing."

- Write a private journal entry about your journey
- Share a brief insight on social media
- Speak up in supportive community spaces
- Create art that expresses your experience

It's completely normal for your healing journey to start as an individual experience or within a small, supportive group, and build from there over time. Healing doesn't have to be shared publicly right away. Take the time you need to process, reflect, and find your voice. When you feel ready, sharing can become a powerful part of your journey.

Each time we share our stories, we help create a world where diverse body experiences are celebrated rather than hidden. Your journey shared authentically and with intention, becomes part of the collective healing we all need.

Nurturing the Seeds of Change: Building Lasting Body Peace

Last night, while reviewing my journey journal from the past year, I found an entry from my early days of body acceptance work. The words reflected such uncertainty and hesitation. Now, looking back, I can see how each small step, each tiny victory, built upon the last to create lasting change. This reflection reminded me that sustainable transformation happens not in grand gestures but in daily choices and consistent practice.

The journey of sustaining positive change requires both patience and strategy. Alexandra, redefined her approach to body acceptance by treating it like tending a garden. "I realized I couldn't rush the process," she shared. "Just like plants need consistent care, my relationship with my body needs daily nurturing." She developed simple routines that supported her growth: morning gratitude practices, evening reflection time, and regular check-ins with her support network.

Building a robust support system becomes crucial for long-term success. Maria created her "circle of trust," a carefully curated group of friends, mentors, and fellow body acceptance travelers who understood her journey. "On days when self-doubt creeps in," she explained, "these are the people who remind me how far I've come and help me stay true to my values." Her experience highlights how community support can anchor us during challenging times.

The practice of regular self-reflection serves as a compass on this journey. Elena developed a monthly check-in ritual where she would review her progress, celebrate victories, and adjust her approach as needed. "I stopped seeing setbacks as failures," she noted, "and started viewing them as information about what needs more attention or a different approach." This flexible, growth-oriented mindset helped her maintain momentum even through difficult periods.

SETTING realistic goals becomes an art in itself. Consider these approaches:
- Break larger goals into daily practices
- Celebrate small victories consistently
- Adjust expectations based on life circumstances
- Focus on progress rather than perfection

Reflection Questions:
What small practices support your body acceptance journey?
How can you strengthen your support network?
What helps you stay committed during challenging times?
How do you measure and celebrate your progress?

The sustainability of positive change often lies in its integration into daily life. Sofia found success by weaving body acceptance practices into her existing routines, adding affirmations to her morning coffee ritual, incorporating gratitude into her evening shower, and finding moments throughout the day to check in with her body's needs.

Remember, sustaining change isn't about maintaining perfect positivity, it's about building resilience and compassion for the journey. As one client beautifully expressed, "Some days I feel stronger in my body acceptance than others, but I no longer see the harder days as failures. They're just part of being human."

Your commitment **to lasting change deserves support and recognition. Consider creating regular check-ins with yourself:**
- Monthly progress reviews
- Weekly celebration rituals
- Daily mindfulness practices
- Regular community connections

The path to sustained body acceptance isn't linear, but with consistent care and attention, the changes you nurture can take root and flourish. Your dedication to this journey not only transforms your own life but creates ripples of possibility for others walking similar paths.

A Sacred Farewell: From My Heart To Yours

Dear Beautiful Soul,

Tonight, as I write these final words to you, I'm sitting in my favorite corner of my home, wrapped in a soft blanket, thinking about our shared journey through these pages. My heart feels full knowing that somewhere, you too might be finding your own cozy spot to read these words. Like you, I've spent countless hours in front of mirrors, fighting battles with my reflection. I've felt the sharp sting of chronic pain on days when simply getting out of bed felt like climbing a mountain. I've carried the heavy burden of trying to fit into a world that sometimes feels too narrow for our beautiful diversity.

I remember the day I finally broke down in my therapist's office, tears streaming down my face, admitting how exhausted I was from trying to be "perfect." My body had been screaming for attention through pain, anxiety, and disconnection. Perhaps you know this feeling too, that bone-deep weariness of trying to be everything for everyone while losing pieces of yourself along the way.

But here's what I've learned and what I want to whisper to your heart: healing doesn't arrive like a lightning bolt. It comes in gentle waves, in quiet moments when you choose to listen to your body's wisdom instead of society's noise. It comes in the morning when you look in the mirror and, instead of criticism, offer yourself a moment of kindness. It comes when you honor your body's needs, whether that's rest, movement, nourishment, or simply permission to be.

Some days, I still struggle. There are mornings when my pain flares up or moments when old doubts creep in like unwelcome guests. But now I know these challenges don't define my worth, and yours don't define you either. Every mark, every curve, every perceived "imperfection" tells a story of survival, resilience, and a life fully lived.

As you close these pages, I want you to know that your journey matters deeply to me. Whether you're reading this curled up in bed, on your lunch break, or in those quiet moments before dawn, you're not alone. Your healing doesn't need to look like anyone else's, it's as unique as the constellations of freckles on your skin or the sound of your laughter.

Take my hand virtually as I share this truth: you are a miracle in motion. Your body, exactly as it is today, has carried you through every storm, every celebration, every ordinary Tuesday. It deserves your gentleness, your patience, and your love.

If you choose to stay connected through my Substack or reach out for additional support, I'm here. But even if our paths don't cross again, know that you carry my deepest hopes for your healing journey. On days when self-love feels impossible, remember that somewhere, I'm holding space for you, believing in your inherent worthiness until you can fully believe it yourself.

Pause for a moment. Place one hand on your heart, the other on your belly. Feel the rhythm of your breath and the steady beat of your heart. This is your body's love song to you, it's been playing all along, even when you couldn't hear it.

In loving witness to your beautiful journey,

Lisa

*The stories in this book reflect the experiences of those I have supported on their healing journeys, including family members, friends, colleagues, strangers, and clients. All names have been changed to protect privacy, and any client words included are shared with their explicit permission.

Bibliography

Ackerman, C. (2023, February 27). Cognitive restructuring techniques for reframing thoughts. *PositivePsychology.com*. https://positivepsychology.com/cbt-cognitive-restructuring-cognitive-distortions/

African Native Tribe. (n.d.). *Neck rings: A cultural symbol of beauty and tradition.* https://african.nativetribe.info/neck-rings-a-cultural-symbol-of-beauty-and-tradition/

Avalos, L. C., Tylka, T. L., & Wood-Barcalow, N. L. (2005). The face of appearance-related social pressure: Gender, race, and socioeconomic status. *NCBI*. https://www.ncbi.nlm.nih.gov/pmc/articles/PMC3662600/

Azevedo, A., & Azevedo, A. (2023). Implications of Socio-Cultural Pressure for a Thin Body Image on Avoidance of Social Interaction and on Corrective, Compensatory or Compulsive Shopping Behaviour. International Journal of Environmental Research and Public Health, 20(4), 3567.

Bernstein, J. (2022, January 25). The connection between mindfulness and body acceptance. *Mindful.org*. https://www.mindful.org/the-connection-between-mindfulness-and-body-acceptance/

Bień, A., Bień, A., Pieczykolan, A., Korżyńska-Piętas, M., & Grzesik-Gąsior, J. (2023). Body esteem and self-efficacy of pregnant women with gestational diabetes mellitus. *International Journal of Environmental Research and Public Health,* 20(3), 2171. https://doi.org/10.3390/ijerph20032171

Borca, A., & Linardon, J. (2020). Cognitive-behavioral therapy for body image and self-esteem. *NCBI*. https://www.ncbi.nlm.nih.gov/pmc/articles/PMC7219979/

Breakfast. http://www.biteofbermuda.com/blog/category/breakfast

Bridging the Gender Gap: Promoting Gender Equality in the Workplace - POSH. https://posh.learnsure.ai/blog/bridging-the-gender-gap-promoting-gender-equality-in-the-workplace/

Cash, T. F., & Smolak, L. (2003). Body perceptions and psychological well-being. *NCBI*. https://www.ncbi.nlm.nih.gov/pmc/articles/PMC11276240/

Cliché Magazine Staff. (2023, March 5). The final frontier of body positivity? Aging gracefully. *Cliché Magazine*. https://clichemag.com/lifestyle/the-final-frontier-of-body-positivity-aging-gracefully/

Cleveland Clinic Staff. (2022, August 8). The benefits of intuitive eating vs. dieting. *Cleveland Clinic*. https://newsroom.clevelandclinic.org/2022/08/08/the-benefits-of-intuitive-eating-vs-dieting/

Dakanalis, A., & Riva, G. (2020). Social media use and body image disorders. *NCBI*. https://www.ncbi.nlm.nih.gov/pmc/articles/PMC8001450/

Donovan, J. (2023, May 12). Diet culture: What it is, its effects, and how to overcome it. *Medical News Today*. https://www.medicalnewstoday.com/articles/diet-culture

Don't Give Up World. (n.d.). *Quote on give up by Alice Walker.* from https://dontgive-upworld.com/quote-on-give-up-by-alice-walker/

Dove. (n.d.). The Dove self-esteem project. *Dove.* https://www.dove.com/us/en/dove-self-esteem-project.html

Feedspot. (2024). Top 90 body positive influencers in 2024. *Feedspot.* https://influ-encers.feedspot.com/body_positive_instagram_influencers/

Fuschia, D., & Nardi, S. (2022). Course and prediction of body image dissatisfaction during pregnancy. *BMC Pregnancy and Childbirth, 22,* 5050. https://bmcpregnan-cychildbirth.biomedcentral.com/articles/10.1186/s12884-022-05050-x

GoodTherapy Staff. (2012, January 30). Body image issues and healthy boundaries. *GoodTherapy.* https://www.goodtherapy.org/blog/body-image-issues-and-healthy-boundaries-013012/

Harvard Summer School Staff. (2023, June 20). Why celebrating small wins matters. *Harvard Summer School.* https://summer.harvard.edu/blog/why-celebrating-small-wins-matters/

Harvard T.H. Chan School of Public Health. (n.d.). Mindful eating. *The Nutrition Source.* https://nutritionsource.hsph.harvard.edu/mindful-eating/

History Hit. (2022, May 5). *The Victorian corset: A dangerous fashion trend?* https://www.historyhit.com/the-victorian-corset-a-dangerous-fashion-trend/

History Skills. (n.d.). *A painful beauty: The history of foot binding in ancient China.* https://www.historyskills.com/classroom/year-7/foot-binding/

JackWilly Main Foswiki. https://wiki.ironrealms.com/Main/JackWilly

Kindful Body. (2022). Six tips for parents to cultivate a body-positive home. *Kindful Body.* https://www.kindfulbody.com/six-tips-for-parents-to-cultivate-a-body-positive-home/

Mayo Clinic Staff. (n.d.). Body dysmorphic disorder - Symptoms and causes. *Mayo Clinic.* https://www.mayoclinic.org/diseases-conditions/body-dysmorphic-disorder/symptoms-causes/syc-20353938

Mayo Clinic Staff. (n.d.). Weight loss: Gain control of emotional eating. *Mayo Clinic.* https://www.mayoclinic.org/healthy-lifestyle/weight-loss/in-depth/weight-loss/art-20047342/

Mental Health Center Kids. (2022, August 8). 120 self-love affirmations for a higher self-esteem. *Mental Health Center Kids.* https://mentalhealthcenterkids.-com/blogs/articles/self-love-affirmations

Mental Health Foundation. (n.d.). Body image in childhood. *Mental Health Foundation.* https://www.mentalhealth.org.uk/explore-mental-health/articles/body-image-report-executive-summary/body-image-childhood

Metricool. (2024). Top body-positive influencers in 2024. *Metricool.* https://metri-cool.com/top-body-positive-influencers/

Morin, A. (2022, February 23). The 4 components of body image. *Psychology Today.* https://www.psychologytoday.com/us/blog/the-savvy-psychologist/202202/the-4-components-of-body-image

Mulcahy, N. (2023, April 13). The impact of body shaming and how to overcome it. *Verywell Mind.* https://www.verywellmind.com/what-is-body-shaming-5202216

Murray, J. (2021, June 30). Racialized beauty standards: A product of colonialism. *The*

Women's Network. https://www.thewomens.network/blog/racialized-beauty-standards-a-product-of-colonialism

National Eating Disorders Collaboration. (n.d.). Media literacy. *NEDC*. https://nedc.com.au/eating-disorders/for-professionals/media-literacy

Neff, K. D. (n.d.). *Self-compassion*. Self-Compassion. https://self-compassion.org

Neff, K. (2023). What is mindful self-compassion? (Incl. exercises + PDF). *PositivePsychology.com*. https://positivepsychology.com/mindful-self-compassion/

Renner, S. (2020, June 8). Mindset matters: The power of positive thinking. *World Campus Blog*. https://blog.worldcampus.psu.edu/mindset-matters-the-power-of-positive-thinking/

Shah, N. (2022, August 19). How your family shapes your body image. *BBC*. https://www.bbc.com/future/article/20220819-the-best-way-to-teach-kids-body-confidence

Silva, W. R., & Do Nascimento, E. (2023). Cultural differences in body image: A systematic review. *Social Sciences, 13*(6), 305. https://www.mdpi.com/2076-0760/13/6/305

The Body Positive. (n.d.). The body positive. *The Body Positive*. https://thebodypositive.org/

The Bump Staff. (2022). How to love your postpartum body. *The Bump*. https://www.thebump.com/a/how-to-love-your-postbaby-body

The Triangle Tribune. (2024). Maryann Black Distinguished Health Equity Symposium. *The Triangle Tribune, 26*(8), 8A.

Tradewinds Fitness. (n.d.). *Nourishing your mind: The importance of prioritizing brain health*. Tradewinds Fitness. https://tradewinds.fit/blog-entry/prioritizing-brain-health/

Tribole, E., & Resch, E. (2022). 10 principles of intuitive eating. *Intuitive Eating*. https://www.intuitiveeating.org/about-us/10-principles-of-intuitive-eating/

Tribole, E., & Resch, E. (2012). *Intuitive Eating: A Revolutionary Program That Works* (3rd ed.). St. Martin's Press.

Tucker, S., & Griffiths, C. (2023). Obesity and set-point theory. *StatPearls*. https://www.ncbi.nlm.nih.gov/books/NBK592402/

Tull, M. (2023, May 29). Challenging negative self-talk. *PsychCentral*. https://psychcentral.com/lib/challenging-negative-self-talk

Victoria & Albert Museum. (n.d.). *Corsets, crinolines and bustles: Fashionable Victorian underwear*. https://www.vam.ac.uk/articles/corsets-crinolines-and-bustles-fashionable-victorian-underwear

Walsh, L. (2021). Love gone wrong: Malignant self-love and narcissism. *BetterHelp*. https://www.betterhelp.com/advice/love/love-gone-wrong-malignant-self-love-and-narcissism/

Wikipedia contributors. (n.d.). *Foot binding*. In *Wikipedia, The Free Encyclopedia*. Retrieved November 22, 2024, from https://en.wikipedia.org/wiki/Foot_binding